on track ...
The The

every album, every song

Brian J. Robb

sonicbondpublishing.com

Sonicbond Publishing Limited
www.sonicbondpublishing.co.uk
Email: info@sonicbondpublishing.co.uk

First Published in the United Kingdom 2025
First Published in the United States 2025

British Library Cataloguing in Publication Data:
A Catalogue record for this book is available from the British Library

Copyright Brian J. Robb 2025

ISBN 978-1-78952-370-6

The right of Brian J. Robb to be identified
as the author of this work has been asserted by him
in accordance with the Copyright, Designs and Patents Act 1988.
All rights reserved. No part of this publication may be reproduced, stored in a
retrieval system or transmitted in any form or by any means, electronic, mechanical,
photocopying, recording or otherwise, without prior permission in writing from
Sonicbond Publishing Limited

Typeset in ITC Garamond Std & ITC Avant Garde Gothic
Printed and bound in England

Graphic design and typesetting: Full Moon Media

Follow us on social media:
Twitter: https://twitter.com/SonicbondP
Instagram: www.instagram.com/sonicbondpublishing_/
Facebook: www.facebook.com/SonicbondPublishing/

Linktree QR code:

on track ...
The The
every album, every song

Brian J. Robb

sonicbondpublishing.com

Would you like to write for Sonicbond Publishing?

We are mainly a music publisher, but we also occasionally publish in other genres including film and television. At Sonicbond Publishing we are always on the look-out for authors, particularly for our two main series, On Track and Decades.

Mixing fact with in depth analysis, the On Track series examines the entire recorded work of a particular musical artist or group. All genres are considered from easy listening and jazz to 60s soul to 90s pop, via rock and metal.

The Decades series singles out a particular decade in an artist or group's history and focuses on that decade in more detail than may be allowed in the On Track series.

While professional writing experience would, of course, be an advantage, the most important qualification is to have real enthusiasm and knowledge of your subject. First-time authors are welcomed, but the ability to write well in English is essential.

Sonicbond Publishing has distribution throughout Europe and North America, and all our books are also published in E-book form. Authors will be paid a royalty based on sales of their book. Further details about our books are available from www.sonicbondpublishing.com. To contact us, complete the contact form there or email info@sonicbondpublishing.co.uk

on track ...
The The

Contents

Introduction 7
See Without Being Seen (1978, 2020) 11
Burning Blue Soul (1981) 19
Soul Mining (1983) 31
Infected (1986) 46
Mind Bomb (1989) 59
Dusk (1993) 72
Hanky Panky (1995) 85
Naked Self (2000) 93
The The Miscellany 105
Ensoulment (2024) 114
Bibliography 128

Introduction

If given his time over again, musician and songwriter Matt Johnson may have chosen a more user-friendly band name for his musical endeavours over the next 45 years. As it was, aged just 17 in 1978, Johnson – at the urging of his friend and early collaborator Keith Laws – chose The The, a name that would confound search engines in the 21st-century internet age. Even Johnson's actual birth name doesn't help much. In a pop music context, there is Jamiroquai's keyboard player, Matt Johnson, and another independent UK-based singer/songwriter also named Matt Johnson! Beyond music, Johnson shares his name with a Canadian actor and film director, an author of paperback thrillers and a Welsh broadcaster!

Asked about the band name in 2006, Johnson was philosophical. Talking to *Chaos Control*, he rather wearily noted: 'It has been raised before and, of course, I have thought about it and received numerous complaints about it, too. Obviously, I cannot change the name of my band at this late stage, but what we have tried to do is to get Sony [owner of the back catalogue] to contact various online retailers to tweak their search engines to accommodate the name. Some have responded to this. It also depends on how you type the name: The The, "The The", 'TheThe'.'

On the other hand – as so often in his lengthy (and, perhaps, underproductive) career – Johnson took a perverse delight in being difficult to find. 'It does make it harder to find unauthorised recordings, bootlegs, [and] free downloads of The The, which I'm quite happy about', he candidly admitted. 'Also, in the internet age when people are becoming increasingly spoilt and expect to find anything [and] everything they want instantly, maybe it's a good thing that The The has gone back to being the underground, word of mouth band it always was? Maybe it's good for people to have to dig around a little to find the things they want rather than having everything served up...?'

Back in 1979, when Johnson was just a teenager, such future concerns were far from his mind. His musical experiments began with reel-to-reel tape, that most analogue of mediums. He began working with overdubbing, combining his vocals with his self-taught musical abilities ('I've always been reluctant to describe myself as a musician in a lot of ways', he told *Tape Op*), in the basement of his parents' pub, The Crown. He quickly turned that experience into a professional opportunity when he secured the position of 'tape op' – a tape operator, or more formally, 'an apprentice sound engineer' – at De Wolfe Studios at the heart of London's Soho, not too far from that city's own Tin Pan Alley, Denmark Street. Eager to impress, Johnson was given permission by his bosses to use his downtime to work on his own music, utilising the studio's equipment.

Across its history, with various combinations of members, The The have never been a chart-storming outfit. By 2024, as the band embarked on their first tour since 2018, accompanying new album *Ensoulment* – the first for 25 years – the band had racked up a mere 52 weeks in the top 75 singles chart, with only seven of those reaching the top 40. The two highest chart hit singles were the *Disinfected* EP (1994), which reached number 17, and the band's political anthem 'The Beat(en) Generation', which reached number 18. Between them, those two records only troubled the singles chart for nine weeks. 'Heartland', the third most-popular single, made it to number 29 and spent 11 weeks in the charts.

It was a different and more successful story with album releases. Both 1989's *Mind Bomb* (number four) and 1993's *Dusk* (number two) made the top five, an improvement on the two earlier albums: 1983's *Soul Mining* (number 27) and 1986's *Infected* (number 14). Even Johnson's typically idiosyncratic album of Hank Williams covers, *Hanky Panky*, made it into the top 30 at number 28. It was all the more disappointing that the sublime 2000 album *Naked Self* – the most recent original album prior to 2024's *Ensoulment* (which reached a respectable number 19) – only made it to number 45 and remained in the chart for a single week. His 1993 song 'Slow Emotion Replay', from his biggest hit album *Dusk*, neatly sums up Johnson's most frequent lyrical obsessions: 'So don't ask me about war, religion, or God, love, sex, or death...'

It's no wonder that Johnson released little new material for the better part of the next two decades, making his small but dedicated following wait. In the first decade of the 21st century, Johnson didn't touch his guitar for seven whole years. However, chart history alone does not do justice to the life and work of a musical creator as complex and conflicted as Matt Johnson.

Johnson was born in 1961, so he was exactly the right age to experience the tail-end of the DIY musical explosion of punk in the mid-1970s. Johnson grew up in pubs with his parents, Eddie and Shirley (of the Blitz generation – not the club, but the Second World War), and three brothers: Eugene, Andrew and Gerard. He and Andrew took advantage of instruments left by guest bands to play at being pop stars. His musical interest was sparked by living above The Two Puddings pub on Stratford Broadway, East London. The place Johnson called home had been notorious for its violence in the 1940s and 1950s, when it was nicknamed the Butcher's Shop thanks to the frequently spilt blood on its white tiles. Growing up, Johnson didn't know that history, but his father, Eddie Johnson, did. He was the landlord of The Two Puddings from the year after Matt Johnson's birth until the pub finally closed in 2000. It was a storied venue that had played host to the likes of The Who, Screaming Lord Sutch (whom Johnson remembered carting a skull with exotic red jewelled eyes around with him), The Small Faces and David Essex, who made his live debut in the pub. As a kid, Johnson was barely aware of who the acts were that his Uncle Kenny (Eddie's younger brother) was signing up to play. From his bedroom, he could hear the glorious noises they made, and wondered – as he drifted off to sleep – what it might be like to be them...

Johnson grew up in an environment in which music was all pervasive, and storytelling was an everyday working-class art form (his father, Eddie, was a frustrated writer – Johnson would publish his memoir *Tales From The Two Puddings* when Eddie was 80). Not allowed in the pub or out onto the Stratford streets, Johnson and his older brother, Andrew, lived in an imaginative world they conjured up in the back yard. The younger Johnson soon joined Andrew at the local school where he was terrorised by aggressive dinner lady 'Mrs Mac' (commemorated in his 2007 song). His younger brother, Eugene, joined the family in 1965, and by 1973, the quartet of brothers was completed with the arrival of Gerard (born on 1 January 1973, and hailed on the BBC's *Nationwide* as the first baby born since Britain entered the Common Market). Three of the brothers – Matt, Andrew and Gerard – would all work together in several artistic pursuits, from music and art to films.

There were other homes (a brief stint in the Suffolk countryside) and other pubs (the haunted 17th-century The King's Head in Ongar, where Johnson attended the local comprehensive). He remembers the first record he ever bought – T. Rex's 'Ride A White Swan', released as a single in October 1970. More interestingly, given his eventual musical evolution, Johnson also recalls buying 1974's *Snowflakes Are Dancing*, Isao Tomita's second album of electronic soundscapes (based on composer Claude Debussy's 'tone paintings') – a sophisticated taste for a 13-year-old.

Johnson's ambitions to make music emerged around the age of 11 in 1972, helped along by a friend from Ongar, Nick Freeston, who had been given a drum kit for Christmas. Johnson had an old acoustic guitar, and he 'appropriated' the family reel-to-reel tape recorder. They were joined in their musical endeavours by a third member, Russell Ball, who, due to his eccentric appearance and proficiency at school, was known as 'the Prof'. Their first efforts consisted of reproducing tracks from The Beatles' album *Help*. They called themselves Roadstar.

By 1974, the Prof was gone, replaced by Brett Giddings, who came with all sorts of exciting new equipment and even some musical competence. As Johnson recalled to biographer Neil Fraser: 'With Brett we went from playing these rather weedy acoustic versions of Beatles songs to playing things like 'Smoke On The Water', 'Black Night' and 'Rebel Rebel', and thinking 'This is great!'' They were joined by a fourth member, Matt Bratby, who had his own bass guitar. Around this time, Johnson got more serious about his musical proficiency and started piano lessons.

'[Roadstar] was my first band. That was a really important part of my life, and they were great guys – there was great camaraderie. The band was a wonderful creative outlet.' The long hot summer of 1976 and the arrival of punk did little to change Matt Johnson's prospects. Roadstar quietly fell apart as its various members left school and found jobs. For Johnson, too, school soon came to an end, and his indifferent academic performance meant his employment options were few. Working from a book titled *So You Want To Be In The Music Business?*, which big brother Andrew had bought for him, Johnson began writing to London record labels, studios and production houses in search of opportunity. Hundreds of letters later, in summer 1977, he scored a lowly job with De Wolfe, a venerable library music house that supplied music to film and television. Based in Soho's Wardour Street, De Wolfe – right next door to the Marquee Club and across the street from the offices of Hammer Films – boasted a well-equipped eight-track recording facility, which immediately drew Johnson's attention. Although a glorified tea-boy, 15-year-old Matt Johnson was in his element.

From his lowly position, Johnson was like a sponge absorbing the analogue technicalities of tape transfer systems and editing. He learned audio tricks – multi-track dubbing, reverse recording, complex edits, tape loops and audio distortion. He quickly came to realise that writing songs and learning to play instruments was just one part of being a musician – if he could conquer the recording studio, he'd be in an entirely new world.

While his parents relocated to The Crown in Loughton, Johnson was broadening his musical education with the encouragement of his De Wolfe colleague Colin Lloyd Tucker, who introduced Johnson to The Velvet Underground, The Residents and Pere Ubu. He also discovered Throbbing Gristle, Cabaret Voltaire and This Heat, all of whom were creating idiosyncratic, distinctive music in a post-punk mode. The punk DIY aesthetic combined with the new sounds made possible by the studio techniques he was learning and the new electronic instruments used by the likes of the earliest 1977 incarnation of The Human League opened up new musical horizons.

The basement cellar of The Crown became Johnson's musical playground, kitted out with second-hand recording gear and instruments. He applied the techniques he'd picked up at De Wolfe to his own homemade recordings in the cellar of the pub. 'I'd heard 'Private Plane' by Thomas Leer, which he did all by himself – all the playing and writing, everything. This was the big turning point because it introduced me to a whole new form of music. Leer had all these drum machines and [tape] loops and totally different instrumentation, and listening to his atmospheric experimentation opened up a whole new world. I realised then that I didn't have to make songs that sounded like everybody else. People could put out a record they had made in their bedroom. That was really inspiring.' By the age of 16, Matt Johnson's musical direction had been set...

See Without Being Seen (1978, 2020)

Personnel:
Matt Johnson: vocals, instrumentation
Produced at Metropolis Studios (2020 remaster)
Producer: Matt Johnson
Label: Cineola (2020)
Chart places: n/a
UK release date: 1 May 2020 (2020 remaster)
Running time: 49:00 (2020 remaster)
All tracks written by Matt Johnson

Recognising the potential of the technology now available, from electronic instruments to advanced studio techniques, the still-teenage Matt Johnson began to think of himself as a one-man band, enabled by the changing way music was made and recorded. It also gave him something else he'd continually strive for: control. That didn't mean he wouldn't work with others (The The would become a catch-all umbrella for Johnson's solo efforts and his output with a band made up of various individuals who would come and go over the next few decades). As early as November 1977, he'd placed an advert in the *New Musical Express* seeking like-minded collaborators: 'Looking for a bass/lead guitarist into Velvets/Syd Barrett.' He received many replies but failed to click with most applicants. One did get through Johnson's reserve: Charles Blackburn, a year older than Johnson and on an extended stay in London from his home in Hull. For the first two months of 1978, the pair collaborated, developing, rehearsing and recording each other's songs. It didn't last – Blackburn eventually ran out of time, money and places to crash, and so had to return to Hull.

Johnson's De Wolfe colleague Colin Lloyd Tucker was also making extensive use of the De Wolfe facilities during downtime to record his own music, overdubbing the instruments himself. He and other De Wolfe co-workers even played some support gigs at various London live music venues under the band name of Plain Characters. Johnson followed Tucker's activities closely, even appearing as a vocalist on a Tucker track, 'Casey's Last Trip' (adopting the band name French Ghosts).

Johnson continued working on his own music in the basement of his parents' pub, bringing the results into De Wolfe to use their facilities to improve the quality of his work. This effort would come together as Johnson's debut album, *See Without Being Seen* – a collection of what he called 'demo tracks' released in limited quantities on cassette in 1979. Recorded in late 1978 and early 1979, Johnson transferred his demos in March 1979 onto quarter-inch tape at De Wolfe, where he had access to a professional graphic equaliser that allowed him to 'fine-tune' his debut. He sold copies at gigs he attended, duplicated onto C30 cassettes – this original release consisted of seven tracks (the 2020 re-release totalled 13).

Writing to a friend, Steve Parry, Johnson noted of *See Without Being Seen*: '[It] deals with you or I (or anyone listening to the songs) as a spectator seeing abstract views of life, be it of people or situations or how people react to various situations and pressures.' The concept of *See Without Being Seen* suggests that of a voyeur, an observer who is himself unobserved. It spoke to Johnson's loner nature, his self-reliance and his self-perception as an outsider, socially, musically and politically. Politics in Britain was lurching rightward with the election of the Conservative government in May 1979. Johnson had grown up in a socialist environment, which – combined with his experiences as a young man in the 1980s – contributed to his avowedly left-wing outlook.

Johnson's musical output was somewhat limited. The tracks on *See Without Being Seen* relied heavily on his Crumar keyboard, his guitar and his growing abilities with multi-track recording and the use of distortion and effects pedals. Disappointed by the results, Johnson lost faith in these early works, although he felt a couple of the songs might have potential. Looking back four decades later, Johnson confessed (in liner notes): 'At my age, I'm well past the point of feeling embarrassed about the accuracy of the tuning, the sloppiness of the timing or the poor technical quality of the recordings. I listen to them now with intrigue, every chord, every note, signifying the baby steps of a mixed-up kid into the world of experimental sound recording.'

Johnson continued to rely only on himself. In between recording sessions, he moonlighted as a bass guitarist with Nick Freeston's pseudo-punk band, then called Cardiac Arrest. In 1978, without Johnson but with Freeston on drums, Gavin Gritton on vocals, Ian 'Haggis' Haggerty on bass and Gary Dawson on guitar, they reformed as Anti-Establishment, releasing a trio of singles produced by The Damned's Rat Scabies.

A second *NME* advert placed in 1979 called for aspirant musicians inspired by Throbbing Gristle and The Residents (he particularly liked their *Duck Stab!* EP), showing how Johnson's musical influences were developing. Response to the ad was disappointing, but it did lead to one significant early partnership. Johnson met with three respondents, but only Keith Laws made enough of an impression. Now a professor of neuropsychology at the University of Hertfordshire, in 1979, Laws was the same age as Johnson and shared many of the same musical tastes. It was Laws who introduced Johnson to the Krautrock music of German experimental bands like Neu! and Faust. Laws also had a collection of instruments and recording equipment that matched Johnson's own, with the addition of early synthesisers. The pair reckoned they had the equipment, ambition and songwriting skills necessary to launch a 'proper' band in a live setting.

'Troops' 2.47
A rudimentary drum machine kicks off *See Without Being Seen*, with distorted, inaudible, echoing vocals humming over the top. Johnson's Crumar keyboard provides a synthy-sounding drone. It's a muddy sound thanks to the

multiple track overlays, but Johnson's main vocals – seemingly describing the thoughts and actions of a military unit – are clear enough. The layering suggests a sonic ambition that, at the age of 17 and with limited equipment and resources, may have actually been beyond the developing artist. It's a short (under three minutes), sharp blast of intent, and elements of the sound mix and the vocals are clearly indicative of the later direction of Johnson's musical creativity. Not so impressed with the actual music when looking back, it is the memories of its creation that stick most strongly with Johnson. 'Despite the imperfections of these recordings, there are very warm memories associated with their creation: my late older brother Andrew (Andy Dog [who contributed illustrations to The The's output]) and I set up our respective small studios in the large cellar of our parents' pub, The Crown ... his for artwork, mine for music. We'd spend so many evenings down there ... we'd sit up late into the night, animatedly discussing future plans, swapping ideas and offering encouragement...' It was in this environment of spirited collegiate collaboration that 'Troops' and the rest of *See Without Being Seen* were created.

'Homa's Coma' 3.51

Opening with Johnson's youthful voice declaring 'take one', 'Homa's Coma' opens with the drum machine running at a more rapid pace. The first hints of rhythm have the unmistakable feel (if expressed much more primitively) of many later The The records, even if the production remains murky. 'Homa's Coma' proves the first instance of lyrics that would recur on more polished recordings. As Johnson hinted at in his liner notes: 'The eagle-eyed may even recognise the odd lyric or melody that ended up appearing on later releases.' The opening lyrics – 'History repeats itself within the realms of my inexperience' – instantly recall the later song 'Icing Up', with Johnson's vocals on this earlier recording repeated almost exactly on the later iteration. Equally, 'See me dwindle, watch me dwell/In my cut out corner, in my plastic world' finds new life, slightly altered, at the end of 'Icing Up': 'See me dwindle, watch me dwell/In my plastic corner, in my plastic world'. Johnson continually reworked and redeveloped some of this earlier material in the early days of the more professional releases under his The The banner. At the age of just 17, Johnson was not only capturing a sense of teen ennui but also capturing the future inertia that would inhibit his career. Recapitulating the punk cry of 'No future!', Johnson penned lyrics like 'I have no future, for I've had no past' – which also found its way into 'Icing Up', a more polished and expanded version of the ideas expressed in 'Homa's Coma'.

'Planetarium' 4.29

'Planetarium' is a frazzled pop song, aggressively played and sung, that – with sharper production – could have held its own against early work from the likes of The Human League or Cabaret Voltaire. From an inauspicious 'plinky plonky' start, 'Planetarium' turns into a much heavier, darker-sounding outing. The driving rhythm provides a suitable backdrop for Johnson's voyeuristic vocals laid over the top. 'I like to watch them', he declares. 'I like to watch them go walking by'. The lyrics have something of the bored teenager in a thankless work environment staring out the window at the people passing – 'I can see everyone, can everyone see?' Other lines suggest an envy about the lives others are living in comparison to the more mundane world of the singer: 'I like to dream about them, the things they do at night'. Johnson even anticipates 21st-century constant surveillance, not least from people compulsively filming each other on phones: 'I like to film them, and see them film me'.

There's definitely something Hitchcockian here – from the obsession with following and watching in 1958's *Vertigo* to the 'peeping tom' nature of Norman Bates in *Psycho* (1960), many of Hitchcock's films featured voyeurism (*Rear Window*, 1954). It's certainly possible that Johnson caught a matinee of one or more of Hitchcock's films and found their themes chimed with his own preoccupations. There's also the question of what exactly the 'Planetarium' of the title is. A planetarium is an educational theatre that recreates views of the night sky. The lyrics 'Me in my room, in my planetarium' suggest that the singer's world is limited entirely to his own teenage bedroom. All he can do is look out, watching others living their lives. There's a strict control on his own emotions, too: 'Controlled elation, fights back again'. As well as the sonic sophistication of 'Planetarium', Johnson also shows signs of developing his lyrical obsessions.

'Spaceship In My Barn' 4.36

An instrument that would become key to much of The The's output makes its first appearance at the opening of 'Spaceship In My Barn' – the harmonica. Above the fuzz of the layered multi-track drums and guitar, Johnson blows his harmonica before it is dropped in favour of his droning vocals. Suggesting a drugged state, the opening lines of 'Spaceship In My Barn' chronicle an out-of-body experience: 'Caught in a dreamlike substance of my choice/open is my head receptive to every voice'. Suddenly, Johnson seems to be anticipating the plot of Steven Spielberg's *E.T.: The Extra-Terrestrial* (which wasn't released until 1982) suggesting he's an alien ready to return to his home-world (perhaps a conscious echo of Bowie's 1970s work?): 'Up is my mind and open to the probe/When will they finally believe I really want to go home?' It's an interpretation suggested by the song's explicit title, which also recalls the Superman comic book mythos, where the Kent family conceal the capsule that brings alien Kal-El to Earth in their Smallville barn. The return of the harmonica and the throbbing rhythm guitar suggest nothing less than Hank Williams, whose songbook Johnson would later cover on the 1995 *Hanky Panky* album.

'Insect Children' 3.51

The opening tribal rhythms of 'Insect Children' immediately call to mind the opening sounds of 'Red Cinders In The Sand', the first track on Johnson's official first album, *Burning Blue Soul*. The off-kilter bass suggests The Doors, while the electronic fizz (especially at the fade) recalls the 1960s experimental electronic pop music of Joe Meek ('Telstar').

Johnson told *Electronic Sound* that some of the titles on *See Without Being Seen* – including 'Spaceship In My Barn' and 'Insect Children' – had been taken from old American comic books. Lyrically, though, 'Insect Children' shows little of that outer space influence. It seems to connect bad behaviour by children – the burning of insects – with the genocidal behaviour of rogue nations, leading to 'Babies burning in their beds, wreathes of fire surround their heads'. It's a hint of the political concerns that would inform the songs on 1989's album *Mind Bomb*, already percolating within Johnson's teen mind.

'My Vymura' 4.30

Throughout the history of The The, there have been three major themes: the frustrations of teenage life (especially in the early material, naturally); political and social issues, inspired by Johnson's lived experience; and songs about various aspects of personal relationships (reduced to the basics of love and sex). The oddly-titled 'My Vymura' is the first 'love' song from Johnson. However, there is no getting away from the fact that the word 'Vymura' is more widely attached to a well-known brand of wallpaper. Perhaps Johnson was hoping for a gig writing advertising jingles? As it is, 'Vymura' appears to be the name of the singer's romantic interest ('My Vymura, how I love her'), a seemingly bright, happy and contented artist. There may be a certain irony in the otherwise bland lyrics, reinforced by the haunting laughter after each chorus, as if the singer doesn't quite believe his own words. The song soon turns to questioning – 'Do do do do, do you love me?' – culminating in a possessive claim of ownership: 'She's mine'. This approach would echo through other The The songs, exploring the uncertainty of love, including the likes of 'The Twilight Hour' on *Soul Mining* and 'August & September' from *Mind Bomb*, culminating in the screaming cry 'You're mine!'.

'Window Ledge' 3.16

Haunting and introspective, 'Window Ledge' builds on the themes of isolation and longing in 'My Vymura'. Lyrically, it's a bit of a mess, talking about hiding in seashells, cooking pies and boxes of Dreft (a laundry liquid!). Amid this word salad, one line does stand out: 'It's the latest sensation, excluding the Pope', a figure Johnson returned to in 'Song Without An Ending' on *Burning Blue Soul*: 'What are we waiting for?/A message of hope/From the Pope'. Hiding here are lines reflecting thematic obsessions echoed in later tracks, like 'I'm not quite as happy as I could have been' and the bitter-sweet 'We fixed up our candlelight, whispering our tunes/Is love the sweetest thing that's happened to you?'

'Window Ledge' concluded the initial cassette release of *See Without Being Seen*. Johnson made an attempt to get his work picked up by a proper record label, to no avail. Talking to Wesley Doyle for *Conform To Deform: The Weird And Wonderful World Of Some Bizzare* [sic], Johnson recalled: 'I spent a lot of time hanging around the offices of various independent record labels, playing my early recordings – tracks from *See Without Being Seen* and the unreleased *Spirits* album – to the likes of Mike Alway at Cherry Red, Ivo [Watts-Russell] at 4AD, Geoff Travis at Rough Trade and Rod Pearce at Fetish Records. I was a teenager, but I was very ambitious and anxious to get going ... I felt I should really start putting records out.' Talking to *Electronic Sound* in 2014, Johnson said the indie labels would at least 'sit and listen to the tapes, [and] encourage me to keep at it', unlike the majors, 'who kicked me back horribly'. None of these approaches paid off, but Johnson was building up contacts who would help him later on, such as Ivo Watts-Russell, who served as a producer on Johnson's *Burning Blue Soul* album in 1981.

'Sugar & Spies' 2.56

For the 2020 expanded CD release of *See Without Being Seen*, Johnson uncovered a further six tracks not included on the 1979 cassette-only release. Long thought lost, the recovered tapes were 'baked' (using an inexpensive food dehydrator), pitch corrected and speed adjusted to be as close as possible to his original intentions. The first of these rediscovered tracks is 'Sugar & Spies', a return to the theme of watching, although in this case, the lyrics are built around the reversed notion: 'I cannot see you'. A pulsing buildup through electronic warbling backs Johnson's echoing vocals. Feedback, programmed drums and whistling synths produce a track unlike anything else in the The The catalogue. It all peters out towards the end, concluding in the detuning 'electronic tonalities' – a credit for the electronic soundtrack of sci-fi movie *Forbidden Planet* (1956), used as composers Louis and Bebe Baron were not members of the Musicians Union – that Johnson often used to wrap up the tracks on *See Without Being Seen*.

'White Stone On Earth' 2.33

During the archival research that uncovered and restored the original cassette release, Johnson also discovered 'quite a few other recordings from the era between the spring of 1978 and the spring of 1979 which, for some reason or other, didn't make it onto the original cassette'. Of these, he noted that 'White Stone On Earth' was 'my first foray into the techniques of Musique Concrète [composition using found sounds] and was inspired by a small book I had purchased at the time: *Composing With Tape Recorders* by Terence Dwyer'.

'White Stone On Earth' shares the minimal lyrics of 'Sugar & Spies', but sonically is very different. The drums sound like someone bashing biscuit tins and tinkling glass bottles, while Johnson exaggerates his 'cockney' accent when declaring such epithets as 'White concrete/Green grass'. There are also other media with what sounds like a Radio 4 broadcast (perhaps the Shipping Forecast, among other news reports) dropped into the background. Feedback and radio tuning noises proliferate. Johnson would return to using media clips in several later songs, but most prominently in the opening of 'Sweet Bird Of Truth' on *Soul Mining* and 'Armageddon Days (Are Here Again)' on *Mind Bomb*. The second half slows the rhythm and ups the radio extracts (possibly from *The Archers*). The whole piece reeks of juvenile experimentation, an attempt at a mixed-media audio creation, but one that wouldn't solicit record label interest. What 'White Stone On Earth' does, though, is suggest that Johnson's interest in using found media extracts to add context to his songs was fully formed as far back as 1978-79.

'People On Sight' 3.37

The slower, gentler 'People On Sight' is hugely interesting for some of its lyrical content. The kind of preset rhythm that turned up later on 'This Is The Day' appears here – Johnson did have an Electro Harmonix Rhythm-12 drum machine, which came with a variety of preset drum patterns. A tempo control sets the pace of each rhythm. The initial drum pattern on 'People On Sight' sounds like one of the Latin settings. Johnson was experimenting with the pattern settings while overlaying keyboard hums and occasional guitar strums. Everything slows down for the end, with the vocals breaking up across the last minute as Johnson's delivery becomes deliberately more hesitant before giving way to aural washes and a brief guitar melody. Of particular interest are the distinctive, notable lyrics: 'Your right is left and your wrong is right/Your white is black and your black is white'. These reversed meanings also form the basis of the first single of 2024 from the album *Ensoulment*, 'Cognitive Dissident'. Written in response to 21st-century culture wars, Johnson includes the evocative lines: 'Left is Right, black is white'. This reveals that even at 17, Johnson's distrust and doubt about the wider world, its credos and ideologies, was fully formed and questioning, a symptom of the rise of Thatcher's Conservatives that would dominate 1980s Britain.

'Let's Do It Again' 3.32

More programmed drumming, changes in tempo and odd foregrounded whistling form the basis of a track that brings Johnson's rhythm guitar work to the fore. Lyrically and musically, it's a doodle, a live-sounding jam that amounts to little. Whistling – as heard here – was a The The staple, although Johnson does indulge in some self-harmonising, something he'd incorporate into future songs. Just as the track fades, Johnson's guitar work goes up a level and starts to sound like something from *Burning Blue Soul*. As with 'Sugar & Spies', this appears to be an experiment where Johnson was getting to grips with his instruments, techniques and vocal possibilities, not necessarily intended to be heard by an audience (or record label executives). As such, it is another curiosity that reveals the roots that would go on to make up the more sublime The The tracks.

'Empty Night Train Home' 5.18

Another obsessive setting for songs or musical vignettes, the late-night train home was something Johnson experienced on a daily basis working at De Wolfe in Soho while living in his parents' pub in Loughton. The daily commute took its toll, and it is no surprise that it should become the subject of one of his earliest songs. There are no lyrics here. Instead, 'Empty Night Train Home' is an attempt to conjure up an atmosphere, one much better realised on 'Diesel Breeze' on *Naked Self*. Johnson's vocal contributions consist of him attempting 'chu-chu' noises and some harmonising with his guitar work, interspersed with a few groans – an attempt to summon the atmosphere of his late-night train ride home in 1978. This approach would later pay off in his city symphony songs on *Dusk*.

'Lazy Finger Shake' 4.07

Both 'Empty Night Train Home' and 'Lazy Finger Shake' reveal that even at this early stage, Johnson was interested in instrumentals, something he would continue to produce for *Burning Blue Soul* ('Red Cinders In The Sand', 'Out Of Control' and 'The River Flows East In Spring'). From its 'whooshing' opening and rudimentary drum machine beats, 'Lazy Finger Shake' meanders along, an indulgent guitar demo that is vaguely Eastern and is clearly a precursor of those later *Burning Blue Soul* instrumentals.

Related Tracks
'Casey's Last Trip' 2.17

Matt Johnson appeared as a guest vocalist on a Colin Lloyd Tucker track, 'Casey's Last Trip' (with the pair adopting the band name French Ghosts), with his contributions instantly recognisable. Included on Tucker's 1984 solo album *Toybox* (recorded in 1978-79, but not released until five years later), Tucker's vocal influence from 1970s David Bowie (and even Syd Barrett) is evident.

Burning Blue Soul (1981)

Personnel:
Matt Johnson: vocals, instrumentation
B. C. Gilbert: guitar ('The River Flows East In Spring')
Graham Lewis: 'karate chop' piano ('The River Flows East In Spring')
Recorded at Blackwing Studios, London; Stage One, London; Elephant Studios, London; Spaceward Studios, Cambridge between the spring and summer of 1981
Producers: Matt Johnson (all tracks), Ivo Watts-Russell ('Song Without An Ending', 'Icing Up', '(Like A) Sun Rising Through My Garden', 'Out Of Control', 'Bugle Boy' and 'Another Boy Drowning'), B. C. Gilbert & G. Lewis ('Time (Again) For The Golden Sunset', 'The River Flows East In Spring'), Pete Maben ('Red Cinders In The Sand', 'Delirious')
Label: Warner Bros., 4AD
Release date: 7 September 1981 (UK)
Charts: UK: 65 (1993 re-release)
Running time: 44:16
All tracks written by Matt Johnson (except where stated)

Looking back on *See Without Being Seen* – his one-man band first collection of songs – Matt Johnson was fairly sanguine about their rejection. 'I can now totally understand why I was turned down by every independent and major label in the country, several times! Despite this, considering I was a self-educated teenager, my confidence was surprisingly high ... I just carried on, feeling inspired and happily creating new recordings, fully convinced that one day my music would find its audience.' One of those who was most encouraging to the teen Johnson was Fetish Records boss Rod Pearce, who saw Johnson's drive and ambition as reason enough to think he'd make progress.

With Keith Laws as a collaborator, Johnson turned his attention to performing live. A fortuitous meeting with Tom Johnston – a decade older than Johnson and Laws, and an accomplished freelance cartoonist with work published in *Private Eye*, *Time Out* and *Sounds* – saw the now two-man The The secure their first live gig. Just days after the victory of the Conservatives in the 1979 UK General Election, The The made their live debut on 11 May 1979 performing at the Africa Centre, third on the bill following Scritti Politti and PragVEC (a band name even more curious than The The, supposedly a contraction of 'pragmatism' and 'vector'). With a gig in the offing, Johnson and Laws decided it was time they had a band name for themselves.

Matt Johnson had previously been operating as a solo artist, with *See Without Being Seen* credited to him (until the 2020 re-release, when it was reclassified as The The). Now teamed with Laws, the pair wanted a band name but had trouble coming up with something to rival The Who, The Beatles or The Knack, who were then currently in vogue with 'My Sharona'. It was Laws who suggested 'The The', intended as a satire of the standard 'The Something' band names. However, cartoonist Tom Johnston may have had a similar idea, as around that time, he sported a badge for a fake band named 'The The'. Johnson felt it was 'a blank canvas ... it didn't pigeonhole us as punk or anything'. He ran the suggested band name by a friend, who pointed out that 'The the' were the final two words of her favourite poem by Wallace Stevens, 'The Man On The Dump'. The full final line read: 'Where was it one first heard of the truth? The the.' To Johnson, this was perfect – it gave an added cultural cache to the name if Johnson ever had to explain its origins to the music press.

For the live performance, Johnson recorded a set of backing tracks at De Wolfe, where he was increasingly concentrating on his own projects rather than on the tasks he'd been hired to perform – by the end of 1979, he'd quit De Wolfe. At the gig, Johnson played guitar and sang vocals, with Laws on his Wasp synthesiser and in control of the backing tapes (drum machine patterns and bass lines), with the duo joined by Peter Fenton Jones – in his sole appearance with the band – on guitar, violin and backing vocals. Steve Parry, in the audience for that debut performance, recalled: 'Their music was a hybrid of electronic drum beats, effected guitar, synths, slabs of noise and distorted vocals.' A second gig followed, with The The (a duo of Johnson and Laws) playing in support of his De Wolfe colleague Colin Lloyd Tucker's Plain Characters.

The still 17-year-old Johnson – through Tom Johnston – became friends with Bruce Gilbert and Graham Lewis, who'd formed Wire in late 1976 with Colin Newman on vocals. Impressed by Johnson's early musical output, Gilbert and Lewis offered The The two support slots during the tour promoting their third album, *154*. Both The The appearances took place at Notre Dame Hall, near Leicester Square – one of which led to their first review in the 1970s music press. Writing in *Record Mirror*, Chris Westwood noted that Wire support bands Vice Versa (later ABC) and The The 'depict the state of modern electronics, dropping sounds over pre-recorded rhythm patterns. Both have their problems in that they lack diversity and variation, and in that their current formula tends to flirt with the one-dimensional.' Despite this damning with faint praise, Westwood felt that The The had 'the facilities to become progressive ... the possibilities of electronics are obvious...' The number-one record in the singles chart at that time – Gary Numan and Tubeway Army's 'Are 'Friends' Electric?' proved the point.

As the 1980s dawned, the newly unemployed Johnson had more time to devote to his musical experimentation, which meant even more hours down in the cellar beneath the pub creating tape loops, rhythm tracks and using his various effects pedals (including a Muff Fuzz, a Small Stone phaser and a Y-Triggered filter, with a Memory Man delay) to distort his guitar licks. Occasional gigs saw Johnson and Laws practice their craft live, playing warehouse parties in the unregenerated Docklands and a birthday party for Toyah Wilcox (whose debut single 'Victims Of The Riddle' hit the Indie Chart in April 1979, and whose breakthrough with 'It's A Mystery' followed in 1981).

The previous summer, Johnson had teamed up with his De Wolfe colleague Colin Lloyd Tucker and John Hyde in The Gadgets, the first fruits of which hit vinyl in March 1980 (Johnson's first appearance on an actual record) with the album *Gadgetree*. Unlike his previous contributions to Tucker's Plain Characters/French Ghosts efforts, Johnson was a fully-fledged member of The Gadgets, contributing both musically and lyrically to the album (18 tracks, with a 44:48 runtime; all tracks credited to Tucker, Hyde, Johnson). Recorded at De Wolfe (where Tucker still worked), both Tucker and Johnson took turns on vocals (Johnson appears on the very The The-like 'There Over There' and 'Devil's Dyke', which features very Johnson-like lyrics). Johnson also got to play with more advanced synthesisers than he'd previously had access to, including a Minimoog and a Prophet 5. An idiosyncratic project, Johnson didn't include his work as part of The Gadgets in his discography, partly due to bad feeling around the later exploitation of the work when The The had built up a reputation. 'There was a studio-only group with Colin Lloyd Tucker called The Gadgets', explained Johnson to Wesley Doyle. 'There was a lot happening. My main memories are of a very creative time. I had very little money, but that was secondary...'

Seventeen-year-old Steve Pearce, known as 'Stevo', contacted the by-now 18-year-old Matt Johnson out of the blue. 'I don't know how he got my number', said Johnson. 'I'd already [been] warned that Stevo was a madman, but I took the call and he asked us to support Cabaret Voltaire at the Porterhouse [in Retford, Nottinghamshire] ... After that, I got more and more involved with him ... Keith Laws and I decided to licence him a track for the *Some Bizzare* [sic] album.' The track 'Untitled' appeared beside early work from Depeche Mode, Soft Cell, Blancmange, B-Movie, Naked Lunch and others – many of whom Johnson knew personally.

Stevo – as young and ambitious as Johnson, and similarly lacking in formal education – started out as a DJ who quickly latched on to the newly emerging electronic music scene. Involved at the birth of the Futurist/New Romantic scene at the cusp of the 1980s, Stevo became a concert promoter, talent manager, established a record label with Some Bizzare, and compiled the Electronic Chart for *Record Mirror* and the Futurist Chart for *Sounds* magazine (which he filled with demos sent to him by bands, many of them unknown). Stevo would be instrumental in the early days of Depeche Mode, Soft Cell and The The.

While Stevo was showing interest in The The, Tom Johnston decided it was time for Johnson to lay down some professional recordings. He booked time at Blackwing Studios, where Depeche Mode made their earliest recordings, and brought in Wire's Gilbert and Lewis as producers. Johnson and Laws turned up with two new tracks: 'Controversial Subject' and 'Black And White'. Tom Johnston took the recordings to 4AD, Ivo Watts-Russell's nascent label, which agreed to release the tracks as a single in August 1980. By that time, The The boasted two new members: Tom Johnston on guitar and Peter Ashworth (later better-known as a rock and pop photographer; he'd taken some of the first commercial photos of Johnson and Laws as a duo) on drums, replacing the tape loops of drum machine patterns (both were credited as band members on that first single release).

In August 1980, Johnson was back at De Wolfe recording tracks for what was intended to be the first album from The The, with the working title of *Spirits*. With Tucker engineering, the band recorded a trio of tracks: 'What Stanley Saw', 'Perspectives And Distortions' and 'Ex Mar Boo'. Johnson also signed a publishing deal with Cherry Red. He was invited to contribute a track to a Cherry Red compilation, so he offered 'What Stanley Saw', but Cherry Red also licensed his song title 'Perspectives And Distortions' for the album title (Johnson had taken the title from an artwork by his brother, Andrew), released in early 1981.

For the first six months of 1981, Johnson developed and recorded tracks intended for his debut album, at that time promised to 4AD. Working in various studios with a series of producers and collaborators – Gilbert and Lewis, Ivo Watts-Russell and Pete Maben – Johnson put together what would ultimately become *Burning Blue Soul*. The album would initially be released under Matt Johnson's own name as a solo work, rather than under The The (it wouldn't be until the 1993 re-issue that the album and the artwork would fall in line with The The's 'brand identity'). Keith Laws – increasingly detached from Johnson's musical project – was put out by this attribution but was barely involved anymore (he claimed credit for the album title and the original psychedelic-style cover art). Laws would later describe the finished record as 'English pastoral psychedelia and Krautrock invention filtered through the hypochondria and religious and cultural allusions of someone whose 19th birthday passed in the summer of 1981. Matt was a magpie.' Although Laws would retreat further from The The (resuming his academic studies), he remained an important sounding board for Johnson right through to the era of *Soul Mining* in 1983.

Before *Burning Blue Soul* was released in the autumn of 1981, Stevo had signed Johnson to a management contract and persuaded him to release a new The The single through his Some Bizzare label. Joined by Laws, Johnson recorded 'Cold Spell Ahead' and 'Hot Ice' at Stage One Studios in Forest Gate, with Pete Maben engineering. Stevo and Some Bizzare were riding high after the success of the label's first single: Soft Cell's worldwide hit 'Tainted Love'. Johnson hoped Stevo would have the same effect on his career as he'd had on Marc Almond's (Johnson would later be part of the revolving membership of Almond's group Marc and the Mambas, playing on their first two albums; Johnson also co-wrote the track 'Untitled' with Almond, which features some The The echoes). During this time, Johnson also met several future collaborators, including J. G. Thirlwell and Manchester-based guitarist Johnny Marr, among others.

Johnson's first album was met with largely appreciative reviews, both in 1981 and following the 1993 re-release under the The The banner. *NME* dubbed the record 'one of the few psychedelic records made in recent years. An acid stew of remarkable proportions.' *Melody Maker* thought Johnson's songs 'explored the joys of melancholy with a nakedness that could only have been equalled by John Lennon on a gigantic existential downer. *Burning Blue Soul* is a bona fide 22-carat desert island disc. It wouldn't be going over the top to say this record stands altogether alone.' For *Record Mirror*, *Burning Blue Soul* offered 'track after track of resonant English multi-dimensional mind-blowing music'. For the reissue, *The Guardian* dubbed the work 'a very strange record indeed [that] at once establishes Johnson as a Great British Eccentric'. In *Select*, Johnson's work was dubbed 'a mixture of clattering instrumentals and deranged ranting sprees. There is no doubting the voice, the vision or the already forbidding atmosphere of paranoia', while *Zigzag* claimed there was 'a subtle uneasiness to the whole album that is both beautiful yet disturbing'.

'Red Cinders In The Sand' 5:42
The opening salvo from *Burning Blue Soul* was the track (as a demo) that sold 4AD's Ivo Watts-Russell on the notion that Matt Johnson was ready to produce his first complete album. The label boss told Neil Fraser that the instrumental was 'as good as anything that was being done by anyone at that time'. One time bandmate Keith Laws (at his online blog) dubbed 'Red Cinders In The Sand' to be made up from 'meandering quasi-orchestral Can and Faust-like tribal rhythmic loops'. Opening with tribal-style drumming over quasi-feedback and distortion, Johnson's voice can be heard muttering about 'hallucinations'. The drum tape loops came from Johnson's days at De Wolfe, with everything filtered through Johnson's collection of effects boxes. Laws noted the rhythms were 'overlaid with sitars, broken guitar sounds and what can only be described as the kinds of brass sounds you hear in epic Roman movies, plus the simple sound of stuff crashing...' Three minutes in, things start building in a more methodical way, still dominated by the drums and horn sound effects. It's a clear example of Johnson's predilection for musical experimentation that would see him produce a variety of finished and unfinished instrumentals (some of which later morphed into completed songs), which ultimately led him to move in the direction of producing music intended for film. Perhaps slightly too long, 'Red Cinders In The Sand' is a statement of intent, opening *Burning Blue Soul* with a blast of sonic psychedelia, both a warning and a promise of the unconventional and diverse tracks that make up the entire album.

'Song Without An Ending' 4:35
The opening track seamlessly transforms into the first vocal offering, 'Song Without An Ending'. Johnson's guitar licks structure the track, with his distorted vocals buried in the muddy mix. The lyrics are drawn from an 18/19-year-old's life in 1981, concerning the existential angst of teen-dom

mixed with current affairs ripped from the headlines (with references to that year's attempted assassinations of both US President Ronald Reagan and the Pope). The monotony of young life would become a major subject, covered by the lyric: 'When everyday of your life, seems the same/as the last and you know who you're gonna meet/and what they're gonna ask/ ... Because we're all caught/up in a mortifying loop/Life!' Keith Laws claimed the opening lines – 'I like you/I think that you're pretty good' – were not about a girlfriend but referred to Johnson's little brother, Gerard, then aged about three. His existential anxiety was reflected in the next lines: 'But I think that you think, that I/Well ... that I'm a bit undercooked...' He also referred to the autodidact he'd become – reading widely through English and French literature, after leaving school with no qualifications at 15 – in the line: 'I'll lie in my bed, feeding my head/Until I become ... fairly intelligent'. These themes would recur throughout Johnson's work, emerging here in first draft form.

'Time (Again) For The Golden Sunset' 3:51
This track, along with 'The River Flows East In Spring', was the fruit of early sessions with Wire members Gilbert and Lewis, recorded at Blackwing Studios. Opening with the classic line 'I used to be indecisive/But now I'm not so sure...', the song exhibits Johnson's first political engagement, exemplified by lines such as 'There's little sign of feeling/When you look into their eyes/The politicians sighing, that/'Nothing's going wrong in our world tonight/Nothing... (we don't understand)". While drawing from the performative politics of the recently-elected Conservative government, Johnson was also focusing on himself and what he was about: 'Am I locked up forever, in a picture of despair/I've put my spirit on to paper and into words/I've opened my eyes and I've realised/Who I really am'.

This plays out against a slowly strummed guitar, atmospheric burbles and echoing rhythms. Recalling the development of the album, Keith Laws noted: 'Matt was not a 'musician' in the traditional sense – he was reasonably comfortable on keyboards, having had some lessons, but most of the time, he stuck to the guitar in an open-E tuning. He was not confident about the songs on *Burning Blue Soul*, and I recall conversations with him about various pieces, which all sounded great to me ... from the prescient musical styles through to the remarkable personal, social and political lyrical voice for someone so young.'

'Icing Up' 7:36
Built from layered guitar tracks, played forwards and backwards, 'Icing Up' was a further development of 'Homa's Coma' on *See Without Being Seen* (one of the first demonstrations of Johnson's ease with reworking older material for new uses), featuring revised lyrics against completely reworked music. Driven by fuzzy guitars, 'Icing Up' runs far longer than the lyrical section. For over five minutes, it becomes an epic example of prog-psychedelia,

developing, dropping and reclaiming each musical strand, dipping in and out of the overdubs that were then Johnson's favourite tool. As it fades out (or seems to, the track slows and starts again across the final two minutes), some of the background drones point forward to much later work on *Dusk*.

Talking to *Uncut* in 2016, Johnson recalled recording the song: 'I went to Cambridge with Ivo [Watts-Russell] to a studio and did 'Icing Up' and 'Another Boy Drowning'. It was done piecemeal in different studios with different engineers. The whole thing was done for £1,800.'

Rarely played live, 'Icing Up' was one of the tracks selected from the back catalogue to feature in the early dates of the 2024 tour that promoted *Ensoulment* – sandwiched between standard 'This Is The Day' and the popular 'Dogs Of Lust'. Reviewing the gig at Collins Barracks in Dublin, John Loftus for *Golden Plec* wrote that 'Icing Up' 'evolves into a psychedelic guitar-driven bliss-out that Neil Young would be proud of', demonstrating that the lengthy instrumental section was still integral to the song as a whole in Johnson's mind and not merely a teenage indulgence.

'(Like A) Sun Rising Through My Garden' 5:01
According to Keith Laws, sections of this track were based around Shennai – a type of music traditionally played at Indian weddings, although back in 1981, Johnson probably thought of his found sounds as being simply exotic and vaguely Asian, fitting in with his general approach to modern psychedelia. It's the most melodic track so far, with the clearest vocals, as if Johnson was becoming more confident in his own performing. Lyrically, Johnson captures the anxiety about a destructive nuclear war that dominated teen minds in the early 1980s: 'World wars and the fate of nations/The sky is glowing with anticipation/I'm wasting away with worry/And my heart just skipped a beat'. The long instrumental break works through several iterations of Indian-sounding noises, ending with the tribal rhythms and horn sounds Laws referred to.

'Out Of Control' 2:01
Another instrumental, 'Out Of Control' was another track from the sessions with Ivo Watts-Russell. The screams and cries that start just as '(Like A) Sun Rising Through My Garden' fades out introduce 'Out Of Control', a guitar-centric riff with scream-like abstract vocals. At only two minutes, it feels like one of Johnson's throwaway musical ideas that he simply never developed into a full song, so he used it as an interstitial piece on *Burning Blue Soul*.

'Bugle Boy' 2:27
Another Watts-Russell production, 'Bugle Boy' was another track where Johnson pulled lyrics from everyday events and news headlines pertinent to the summer of 1981. Riots around England – in Brixton, Toxteth, Chapeltown and Handsworth – saw Johnson mix current affairs with personal affairs in

the opening: 'The country is riddled with social ills and aches/But my heart is calmed by her embrace'. His position as a singer-songwriter increasingly engaging with political content only served to increase Johnson's sense of ennui – there was little he, a mere singer, could do about the state of the world except lament it in verse. Some of the lines came from direct experience, notably: 'This strange little boy said/'Mister, play us your guitar'/ and I said 'No... I can't'/and put my guitar in the car'. Talking to journalist Pat Gilbert, when *Burning Blue Soul* was reissued in 1993, Johnson admitted: 'That actually happened. I was walking out of the door of the pub I lived in [The Crown in Loughton], and some kid said it to me.' Johnson looked back at the incident with some regret: 'Later, I thought I should've [played]. If I considered myself a singer-songwriter, I should have sat and played for him, but I didn't. I'm a bit shy.'

Opening with the sound of a simulated hunting horn (possibly from the De Wolfe library) – as if to justify the title – 'Bugle Boy' is another guitar-driven track with a simple but very effective refrain. Despite the heavy treatment of the vocals, the lyrics are clearer than many of those on *Burning Blue Soul*. It also sees the first appearance of the line 'I was trapped in the triviality of everydayness', a phrase from philosopher Heidegger that Johnson probably encountered reading Colin Wilson's *The Occult*. 'Bugle Boy' ends with a *Twilight Zone* kick with the final couplet 'Who can save us now/The world rots/I did know the secret of the universe/Only I forgot!', which is both pretentiously profound and tremendously funny.

'Delirious' 3:33

Engineer Pete Maben co-produced 'Delirious' during the same session that resulted in opening track 'Red Cinders In The Sand'. It's a driving, anthemic track that smashes a lot into three-and-a-half minutes. The lyrics are a mix of self-referential process thoughts about 'meaningful songs', capturing 'the unspoken feelings of my heart' and pointless 'playing around with this stupid guitar'. There's an interest in the changing seasons and the effect they have on the libido (evident across *Burning Blue Soul*, and something that would recur throughout The The's oeuvre, including in such tracks as 'August & September' and 'Kingdom Of Rain' on *Mind Bomb*, 'Love Is Stronger Than Death' on *Dusk*, 'December Sunlight' on *Naked Self* and in both 'I Hope You Remember (The Things I Can't Forget)' and 'A Rainy Day In May' on *Ensoulment*).

After a minute, the tone and tempo change, as Johnson duets with himself with different vocal treatments. A reference to 'insect fear' perhaps recalls 'Insect Children' on *See Without Being Seen*. Johnson's self-flagellation regarding his own inadequacies continues well into the fade where these lines can barely be made out: 'You're at an age when/You should be feeling good/But when you hide in your bed/And look in your head/You find you've gone/Deeper than you should'.

'The River Flows East In Spring' 3:33
Third of the instrumentals on *Burning Blue Soul*, 'The River Flows East In Spring' was produced by Gilbert and Lewis and saw Bruce Gilbert playing guitar while Graham Lewis handled the 'karate chop' piano section. The piano kicks in after about a minute, along with rhythmic handclaps, which supplant the ethnic chanting (another of Johnson's treasured experimental tape loops, either from De Wolfe or the cellar of The Crown). It makes for a hypnotic mix of atmospheres and tensions that evolve, shape-shifting and switching form. It culminates in a rather sinister guitar riff suggesting a thriller or horror film before things peter out. 'The guys from Wire took me under their wing', Johnson told *The Quietus*:

> Bruce Gilbert and Graham Lewis produced the first The The single ['Controversial Subject'/'Black And White'] and a couple of tracks from my *Burning Blue Soul* album. I went on to work with Mike Thorne, who's the producer of [Wire's album] *154*, [and] who produced 'Uncertain Smile' in New York, and Paul Hardiman – who was the engineer on *154* – who became my co-producer on *Soul Mining*. Plus, I supported [Wire vocalist] Colin Newman. So, there's huge interaction between The The and Wire around this period.

'Another Boy Drowning' 5:53
The riots and civil unrest of the summer of 1981 – featured on 'Bugle Boy' – also informed 'Another Boy Drowning'. Talking to Journalist Helen Fitzgerald about *Burning Blue Soul*, Johnson addressed the inspiration for the lines: 'There's people on the street/Throwin' rocks at themselves/Coz they ain't got no money/And they're livin' in Hell'. Said Johnson: 'It really annoyed me – there were kids of 11 and 12 being egged on by extremist organisations who were capitalising on local unrest.' In an uncanny echo of those long-ago days, as The The were rehearsing for their *Ensoulment* tour, further 'unrest' unfolded in the English riots of the summer of 2024, just as the government changed from Conservative to Labour for the first time since 1997. Looking back on 'Another Boy Drowning', Johnson saw it as marking a change in his songwriting, a more considered take on the personal and the political that would inform much of his subsequent albums. For the final track of his debut album, Matt Johnson had finally found his voice.

Related Tracks
'Controversial Subject' 2.50 (Johnson, Laws – credited as The The)
Produced by Wire's Bruce Gilbert and Graham Lewis and released in August 1980 on 4AD, 'Controversial Subject' was the first single from The The – and it very much sounds of its time. The band lineup was Johnson on instruments and vocals, 'Triash' (Peter Ashworth) on drums, percussion and vocals, Tom Johnston on guitar and vocals, with Keith Laws on synthesiser and vocals –

the most expansive lineup the band had featured to that point. 'I released [this] single before I was 18', Johnson told *Uncut*. 'I was anxious to get on with things.'

Primitive though the sound may be, the roots of the future direction of The The can be discerned in 'Controversial Subject', even if Johnson would not go down the multiple vocalist route again (it makes for a crowded-sounding record). The track was played on John Peel's late-night Radio 1 show and became part of the band's then-limited live repertoire. A review of a gig at London's Rock Garden (anonymously quoted in Neil Fraser's *Long Shadows, High Hopes*) liked the band's live sound, mentioning 'Controversial Subject' in particular: 'You could almost call it psychedelic ... True, the vocals could have been stronger and little things need polishing, but ... with more time and experience, [The The] could be interesting.' It was re-released as part of a *Radio Cineola* podcast (in which Johnson explores his own past work) in 2010.

'Black And White' 3.24 (Johnson, Laws – credited as The The)
The B-side to 'Controversial Subject', 'Black And White' continued the strained, chanting vocal style of the A-side. Longer than the single's main cut, this track perhaps reflects more heavily the input of Gilbert and Lewis, with it sounding similar to their own post-Wire output under the name Dome. The lyrics feature Johnson's interest in opposites (black and white) – later to develop into his focus on the changing of language so that words mean their opposite (as on 'People On Sight' on *See Without Being Seen* and – much later in 2024 – on 'Cognitive Dissident' from *Ensoulment*). Vocally, Johnson sounds a bit strained – presumably on purpose and in an attempt to imitate some of the other post-punk bands of the period. Towards the end, it descends into the kind of hand-clapping-driven instrumental track of the sort that featured throughout *Burning Blue Soul*.

'Untitled/Strawberry Sunset' 3.17
A step up from the previous two songs, 'Untitled' engages with contemporary news stories, mentioning the Sunday papers and a perennial subject they focused on in the 1970s and 1980s, the Moors murderers: 'All this and more/ All this and the Moors murders'; 'Ice cream in the sun/I scream in the Sunday papers'. A monotonous rhythm guitar line gives the piece structure as Johnson's seemingly random vocals drop in and out. Steve Parry of Neu Electrikk recalled:

> Musically, the *Some Bizzare* album was pretty horrible. Lots of the music was recorded cheaply in local recording studios. I was in the studio for the recording of The The's 'Untitled' contribution. It was a disastrous [recording] session because the engineer did not like Matt or Keith at all. He made it plain he thought they were a couple of wankers. Obviously, [they] picked up

on this, which wasn't good for creativity, so I ended up at the mixing desk doing what the engineer should've been doing. I think I played a little bit of guitar, too, but I'm not credited. The track was originally called 'Strawberry Sunset', but when the tape came back, the engineer had crossed that out and in its place written 'The Bollock Song'! Because nobody was particularly pleased with the session, the reel-to-reel tape ended up in my possession ... I had it for months, nobody wanted it ... The track ended up [on the *Some Bizzare* album] as 'Untitled'.

The two sides of the Some Bizzare record were labelled Fish and Eye Lamp (a typical Stevo/Some Bizzare eccentricity). The The appeared on the Fish side, sandwiched between Depeche Mode's 'Photographic' and B-Movie's 'Moles'. Writing in *SALT* #9 (2011), Kevin McCaighy noted:

For decades, The The's 'Untitled' has been one of the most notorious and dismissed tracks of the band's early output, not least in the opinion of Johnson himself. But its heady mix of electronic rhythms and eccentric wordplay is a valuable example of post-punk experimentation. Johnson's double-tracked vocal loops relentlessly around Keith Laws's WASP synth shapes, with Johnson (and an uncredited Steve Parry) playing fuzzed guitar, burbling into something quite outside of what the band would later achieve. It deserves to be valued far more than as a curio.

Writing in *Sounds* in January 1981, 'Betty Page' (Beverley Glick) put The The's effort into the 'whimsical confection dept.', noting 'The The might appear moody and gloomy on first hearing the creeping bassline, but the wordplays are the highlight.'

'What Stanley Saw' 2.53
Included on the 1981 Cherry Red compilation album *Perspectives And Distortions* (under the Matt Johnson moniker), 'What Stanley Saw' was the first track from the unreleased 1979 *Spirits* album to see the light of day. Recorded in the spring of 1980 at De Wolfe, Johnson performed all the instruments with his De Wolfe colleague Colin Lloyd Tucker engineering. Suggesting a 'What The Butler Saw' salacious storyline, the title instead appears to be a juvenile play on the 'Stanley 3-in-1 saw' DIY tool... From the Morse Code sounds of the opening through the thrilling guitar riff, pulsing percussion, Biblical references and references to atomic warfare and frustrated romance, 'What Stanley Saw' comes across as a first draft of many later The The songs.

'Cold Spell Ahead' 3.55
When Stevo's Some Bizzare label accidentally hit the big time with the UK number-one single 'Tainted Love' from Soft Cell, a follow-up was quickly

needed. After recording *Burning Blue Soul* for 4AD, Johnson switched his allegiance to Some Bizzare, starting with a one-off deal for the single 'Cold Spell Ahead' – it would prove to be the first draft of a pivotal The The song. In the spring of 1981, Johnson and Laws reconvened to record two tracks (the other being the B-side 'Hot Ice') for Some Bizzare's second single release. The pair set up shop at Stage One in London's Forest Gate, taking advantage of the availability of equipment left behind by Mute Records founder Daniel Miller, who'd been working with Depeche Mode, namely a Korg KR55 drum machine and an ARP sequencer. As an inadvertent result, 'Cold Spell Ahead' ended up with a similar rhythm track to Depeche Mode's 'Photographic' (the faster *Some Bizzare* album version rather than that featured on their debut LP *Speak & Spell*). With Pete Maben engineering, the new song steered clear of some of the multi-track overdubbing and layering, reverb and fuzzy guitar effects that had dominated *Burning Blue Soul*. A much cleaner vocal approach was the result, with the lyrics being essentially the same as the later 'Uncertain Smile', complete with a humming middle break. The 'Cold Spell Ahead' version was a Frankenstein mash-up of two entirely separate songs, with the opening section being the first two verses of what would become 'Uncertain Smile' (lacking the final line 'Uncertain emotions force an uncertain smile').

The second song, called 'Touch Of Experience', comes in following the humming section, a much darker song playing out at a different tempo, before switching again to an extremely short, first-draft version of the piano finish famously played by Squeeze keyboardist Jools Holland on the re-recording. Johnson doesn't remember why he forced these two tracks together, except for the fact that he needed a single for Some Bizzare. 'I think I had the two songs; they were going to be two separate songs, and maybe I couldn't find a part to that outro? I've never done anything like that since, changing the tempo and the key at the same time. I did want to turn that end section into its own song, but never got round to it.'

'Hot Ice' 5.35 (Johnson, Laws)
A cacophony of sound, with strummed guitars, clattering percussion and thrumming sirens, 'Hot Ice' was credited as a co-write between Johnson and Laws. In fact, this and 'Cold Spell Ahead' signalled the end of their partnership. 'When we recorded [these tracks], Keith [Laws] was doing less and less. I was pretty much writing and playing everything. Keith's interests lay elsewhere, I guess … I was working in my own studio, and writing, and really coming on in leaps and bounds.'

Soul Mining (1983)

Personnel:
Matt Johnson: vocals, synthesisers, percussion, various instrumentation, chant on 'GIANT'
Harry Beckett: trumpet on 'Perfect'
Paul Boyle: fiddle on 'This Is The Day'
Andy Duncan: drums on 'This Is The Day', 'Uncertain Smile', 'Soul Mining' and 'Perfect'
Camelle G. Hinds: bass guitar on 'I've Been Waitin' For Tomorrow (All Of My Life)', 'Uncertain Smile', 'The Twilight Hour', 'GIANT' and 'Perfect'
Jools Holland: piano on 'Uncertain Smile'
David Johansen: harmonica on 'Perfect'
Keith Laws: melodica on 'Three Orange Kisses From Kazan'
Thomas Leer: synthesisers on 'I've Been Waitin' For Tomorrow (All Of My Life)', 'The Twilight Hour' and 'GIANT'
Martin McCarrick: cello on 'The Twilight Hour'
Zeke Manyika: drums on 'I've Been Waitin' For Tomorrow (All Of My Life)', 'The Twilight Hour' and 'GIANT', chant on 'GIANT'
Jeremy Meek: bass guitar on 'The Sinking Feeling'
Steve James Sherlock: flute and saxophone on 'Three Orange Kisses From Kazan' and 'Waiting For The Upturn'
Anne Stephenson: violin on 'The Twilight Hour'
Frank Watt: sticks on 'GIANT'
'Wix' (Paul Wickens): accordion on 'This Is The Day'
Recorded at Mediasound (New York), The Garden (London), Advision (London), SARM (London) between 1982 and 1983
Producers: Paul Hardiman, Matt Johnson
Label: Some Bizzare (UK)/Epic (US)
Release date: 21 October 1983 (UK)
Charts: UK: 27, Aus: 70, Canada: 22, Netherlands: 14, New Zealand: 16
Running time: 41:42
All tracks written by Matt Johnson

Beguiled by Stevo Pearce and the possibilities of his Some Bizzare record label – especially in the wake of the success of Soft Cell with 'Tainted Love' – Matt Johnson was only too eager to sign up. With promises of a major label deal, he quickly got to work developing songs that would form his second album – and he already had a title. Johnson had picked up the phrase 'the pornography of despair' from his older brother Andrew, who had come across it in art criticism. Andrew Johnson had painted the phrase into his own artwork. Building on the breakthrough he'd achieved, lyrically and musically, on 'Another Boy Drowning', Johnson now adopted more traditional song structures.

The first fruits of Stevo's efforts were a handshake agreement with London Records – part of Phonogram – to develop and re-record 'Cold Spell Ahead' as a single. While Johnson was laying down demos, he was summoned to New York in May 1982 to work with 'Tainted Love' producer Mike Thorne. There was no written contract, just a verbal agreement, which proved enough for London Records to pay for the project. Johnson and Thorne worked at Mediasound on West 57th Street, with Johnson taking up residency for the duration in the Mayflower Hotel on Central Park, on London Records' dime. Johnson recalled: '[Stevo] did what I refer to as a Tin Pan Alley sleight of hand deal. He got them to pay for me to go to New York, which was an expensive affair with a good studio and a nice hotel. And he got them to do this without anything in writing.'

Johnson dumped the second half of 'Cold Spell Ahead' (the 'Touch Of Experience' section) and focused on the more commercial first half. He had access to much more sophisticated equipment than he'd used on *Burning Blue Soul*, including a Roland 808 drum machine, Thorne's Fender Precision bass and a Rickenbacker 12-string guitar that supplied the main riff on 'Uncertain Smile'. An early digital synthesiser, the Synclavier, was used, and session musician Crispin Cioe from the Uptown Horns provided the saxophone and flute lines. New to Johnson was the Xylorimba (sometimes referred to as a xylo-marimba or a marimba-xylophone) – essentially a five-octave range xylophone once popular in American vaudeville. Used by many composers, including Alban Berg, Pierre Boulez, Olivier Messiaen, Krzysztof Penderecki and Karl Stockhausen, its first use in pop in the 1980s seems to have been on the intro section to this first version of 'Uncertain Smile'.

As soon as the now 20-year-old Stevo heard the result of Johnson's New York recording session, he forgot all about London Records and began touting 'Uncertain Smile' around the major labels. Talking in 2014, Johnson still backed Stevo's move. 'I didn't really like London Records', he told John Doran at *The Quietus*. 'I didn't find them that friendly. They were more of a British pop label.' Stevo arranged an unlikely bidding war, resulting in Johnson willingly signing with US giant CBS, especially given their past track record. 'Suddenly, it was Bob Dylan, Leonard Cohen, Johnny Cash – that's where I wanted to be. So, I was delighted.' The deal was done and Johnson was suddenly £70,000 richer (minus Stevo's management fees) – he promptly bought himself a flat in Stoke Newington, and still had plenty left over. All he had to do now was deliver an album that fulfilled the promise of 'Uncertain Smile'.

In the second half of 1982, Johnson's life was all set to 'surely change' (as he later expressed it in 'This Is The Day'). He appeared on the cover of *Sounds* and was interviewed in *Melody Maker*. Pre-release copies of the extended 12" of 'Uncertain Smile' were being widely played in clubs. He began a personal (and later professional) relationship with Dundee-born Fiona Skinner, a Thames Television graphic designer he met at BBC TV Centre when Soft Cell were performing 'Bedsitter' on *Top Of The Pops*.

Problems were looming, though. 'At this point, I was working in my own time on *The Pornography Of Despair*. I was signed on the strength of

'Uncertain Smile', which was the most commercial thing I'd ever done ... in fact, it was the most commercial thing that I'd probably ever do. So, when they heard everything else I'd recorded, [CBS] probably thought, 'What the fuck is this?" Having met with a negative response from CBS to *The Pornography Of Despair* and personally dissatisfied with the quality of the material he'd produced, Johnson started from scratch to create what would become *Soul Mining*.

Soul Mining would see Johnson involving a rotating group of artists in his work. As a band, The The never had a stable lineup; it was an ever-changing group of musicians, their participation dictated either by the requirements of individual songs or by Johnson's interest in their work, or even simply through personal friendships. The only consistent member of The The from the beginning was to be Johnson himself.

Those involved in making *Soul Mining* included his first partner in the band, Keith Laws, his much-admired predecessor and pioneer, Thomas Leer, Orange Juice drummer Zeke Manyika, New York Dolls member David Johansen and Jools Holland, among several others. Some of these – like Manyika – would feature on subsequent The The albums (in Manyika's case, on *Infected* and *Dusk*). The entire package was produced by Johnson and Paul Hardiman. 'I was just a teenager when I wrote some of the songs on *Soul Mining* ... it [was] all instinctual, just how you feel,' Johnson told *Uncut* in 2016. Talking with *Electronic Sound* in 2014, Johnson noted: 'It is quite a personal set of songs. Someone once said it was a record for small rooms but big imaginations.'

CBS summoned Johnson and Thorne back to New York in October 1982 for further recordings, and this time, Johnson was accompanied by Some Bizzare's Stevo. His presence would not be helpful. Johnson suffered a crisis of conscience – having recently come into money, he doubted his ability to sing about the poverty and deprivation he saw around him, which had been the subject of such earlier songs as 'Bugle Boy' and 'Another Boy Drowning'. Encouraged by Stevo to sample New York's low life in search of inspiration, the pair went on a multiple-day drug bender. This was followed by an unauthorised road trip to see 'the real America', taking in Detroit.

This second experience in New York saw Johnson coming to terms with his new status as a 'professional' recording artist, one with obligations to his record company and his potential audience. It served to clear his head. It also demonstrated that working with an established producer like Thorne was not the way forward. Instead, Johnson settled on Thorne's former engineer, Paul Hardiman, to help him realise *Soul Mining*. This would allow Johnson to take on the role of co-producer, exercising a high degree of control. 'I had decided that, from now on, I would co-produce my albums', said Johnson. 'I knew my way around the recording studio and I also knew exactly how I wanted my songs to sound. In fact, writing songs wasn't just the music but also the sound that I'd been working out in my head. I needed a creative foil, rather than an engineer for hire. The ideal situation would be to find talented, ambitious engineers, who I would offer a co-production credit to, rather than established producers, who were often set in their ways and quite controlling.' It was Hardiman's creative involvement with Johnson that would transform the unsatisfactory work he'd done on *The Pornography Of Despair* into the album that announced the arrival of The The: *Soul Mining*.

In *Sounds*, critic Dave Henderson lavished *Soul Mining* with praise, awarding it five stars, calling it 'a classic slice of everyman's everyday music, ready for the radio, the dance floor and those thoughtful interludes late at night.' While *NME* had given single release 'This Is The Day' a poor review, Don Watson was more positive about the album, suggesting Johnson's lyrics exhibited 'rare literary flair. More importantly, he has the command of music's immense possibilities to carry them through without self-indulgence.' According to *City Limits*, 'Johnson harnesses the ordinary, the passionate, the familiar and the unknown to come up with tough, anxious, but romantic songs.' The US music press was equally welcoming, with *Rolling Stone* noting that Johnson stood out thanks to 'his sense of structure and unerring ear for sonic definition.' With five weeks in the UK Album Chart, *Soul Mining* reached a high of number 27, but was certified Gold in the UK in 2019.

'I've Been Waitin' For Tomorrow (All Of My Life)' 5:45
Opening track 'I've Been Waitin' For Tomorrow (All Of My Life)' presents an upbeat sound combined with defiantly downbeat self-coruscating lyrics. A sampled countdown (followed by rocket take-off effects – perhaps inspired by the then-recent arrival of US nuclear weapons on British soil) sets the scene perfectly (although the number seven is mysteriously missing or muted). The song is an energetic cry from the heart, tackling subjects as widely diverse as unrequited love, the political situation, the nature and effect of propaganda and the lack of a hopeful tomorrow. Political propaganda was a subject that Johnson was interested in. He told *Uncut* that this song was 'about cognitive dissonance. About this world that's constructed for us by the media. You're experiencing one thing in your life, and then the institutions and news services that you think you should trust are all showing you something completely different. So, there's the internal conflict and confusion.'

Johnson's desperation is expanded by a penetrating drum line from Manyika and driving synths from Johnson's one-man-band pioneer hero Thomas Leer. Initially, the vocal comes in just over the percussion, so it's only with the arrival of the chorus that the rest of the instrumentation kicks in. More sampled American-accented voices appear, uttering 'it's working ... keep talking'. Johnson declares himself to be 'Another year older and what have I done/My aspirations have shrivelled in the sun', a self-critical note that would recur in other songs. Love has failed ('the cancer of love has eaten out my heart'), while political propaganda has taken root ('I've been filled with useless information/Spewed out by papers and radio stations'). This thought transforms into cause and effect – 'My mind has been polluted/And my energy diluted' – connecting the political and the personal. It's a shockingly dark sentiment, but – oddly – the driving aggression makes it more palatable. It was a sound that Johnson would build upon further with many of the tracks that make up *Infected*.

'This Is The Day' 3:42 (Single) 4:59 (Album)
Probably the band's best-known, most widely heard track, the ubiquity of 'This Is The Day', the third single from *Soul Mining* (2 September 1983), is largely due to its use in film and television. It spent four weeks on the chart (just like 'Uncertain Smile'), peaking at number 71, four short of the high that 'Uncertain Smile' reached. It was also the first The The track to be accompanied by a bespoke music video.

Johnson was free of Thorne's insistence on the use of his Synclavier on 'Perfect', and was able to use the Suzuki Omnichord he preferred, giving the track a unique sound. The opening notes, situated neatly behind the accordion (another unusual instrument for pop, played by Paul 'Wix' Wickens; there's also a fiddle, from Paul Boyle), stem from the Omnichord (also heard on 'The Nature Of Virtue') and give the track a lightness of touch that Johnson developed as his unique sound, despite the grimness of much of his lyrical content. Johnson told The Best Line of Fit in 2024: 'One thing I've always tried to do in a lot of my songs is if the lyrics are a bit dark, the music has to be joyous because I don't want to listen to depressing music with depressing lyrics.' The lyrics here match the upbeat, if melancholy, nature of the music. His life had changed considerably on the day the CBS contract was signed (although that would come back to haunt him), bringing him money, an outlet for his music, a new relationship and, eventually, his first flat.

It would be Skinner who would put together the second music video for 'This Is The Day', featuring a compilation of images reflecting Johnson's memories of his own life from childhood (he was only 21 at the time) and pictures from their own relationship. The first video (directed by Tony Dow) was such a disappointment to Johnson, featuring an awkward green-screened performance, that he had it withdrawn from circulation for 40 years. 'As the years have advanced, my feelings towards the video have softened and I can see the funny side of it – particularly my haircut and the way I'm self-consciously skulking around! More poignantly, all my immediate family are in it; only two of us are now left...'

Johnson has come to see 'This Is The Day' as his most impactful work. 'It wasn't one of those songs that you'd consider a hit single, but over time, it's been used in films and adverts in America. It's by far one of my most successful songs in terms of the money that it's generated ... It seems to be a song that people absorbed into their emotional landscape.' The first use of the song in a film came with Mark Romanek's cult movie *Static* (1985), after which its use proliferated, including on *Empire Records* (1995), *Every Day* (2018), *I Feel Pretty* (2018), and on television in *Sex Education* (2019), *Jett* (2019), *The Deuce* (2019) and *WeCrashed* (2022). Its widest use was in *Guardians Of The Galaxy Vol. 3* (2023). It also turned up in adverts, most notably on a series of animated M&Ms spots, and through constant repetition, it made its way into the consciousness of Americans. It was still being used in 2024, turning up in an episode of Alan Carr's autobiographical comedy-drama *Changing Ends*.

'The Sinking Feeling' 3:44

The thoughts that informed 'I've Been Waitin' For Tomorrow (All Of My Life)' return on 'The Sinking Feeling', combining ineffectual lethargy with a polluted mind and connecting both to the political reality of the early 1980s: 'I'm just a symptom of the moral decay/That's gnawing at the heart of the country' is one of the greatest couplets of the 1980s. Johnson wrote the lyrics just before the ten-week, 74-day Falklands War of April, May and June 1982 that did so much to get Margaret Thatcher re-elected in 1983 in a wave of patriotic English populism, with a landslide and over 42% of the vote and an increase in MPs (as the opposition vote split between Labour and the SDP-Liberal Alliance).

Again, Johnson expressed his pessimism about the future of Britain in his lyrics, while presenting his sentiments in an uplifting musical package, featuring Jeremy Meek on bass guitar. Somehow, Johnson hit on the trick of conveying his pessimistic and downbeat lyrics in an upbeat, positive-sounding musical arrangement, all the better to get his messages across. It was a subversive approach to pop that gathered him few accolades (or, at least, not until decades later). Set against clapping hands percussion, Johnson sings out his despair, while jangly guitars and Meek's distinctive bass sound provide something akin to hope. Self-destruction, however, is not the answer ('You can't destroy your problems/By destroying yourself'), but the modern 1980s right-wing vision of Britain's future appears to be inescapable: 'Tomorrow's world is here to stay/They wouldn't have it any other way'. It was an oppositional stance that Johnson would continue to take in songs like 'Heartland' (on *Infected*) and 'The Beat(en) Generation' (on *Mind Bomb*), with increasing ferocity.

'Uncertain Smile' 4:56 (Single) 6:52 (Album)

Developed from the earlier 'Cold Spell Ahead', the first single released (in October 1982) under the banner of The The was recorded in two distinct versions of this ever-changing song. The first half of that earlier song provided the basis for the initial revision, but it required expansion, both musically and lyrically. Opening with the distinctive sound of the Xylorimba (purchased by Johnson from Manny's Music on Manhattan's 48th Street), the original New York recording of the single version of 'Uncertain Smile' marks its difference from its predecessor immediately. An upbeat, optimistic guitar sound takes over, with a solid drum underlay courtesy of the Roland drum machine. Johnson's vocal delivery is clearer and more assured than on 'Cold Spell Ahead'. Despite the lyrics referring to romantic obsession, the track maintains an upbeat atmosphere. The key lyric – 'A broken soul stares from a pair of watering eyes/Uncertain emotions produce an uncertain smile' – is at best ambivalent, while the music is uplifting, making for the perfect contrast. Sticking out like a sore thumb (compared to the 1983 re-recorded version) is Crispin Cioe's sax and flute work. The roots of the later added Jools Holland piano solo are there in both 'Cold Spell Ahead' and this initial version of 'Uncertain Smile', but it is clear neither Johnson nor his producer here, Mike Thorne, know quite what to do with this section or how to end the tune other than through a stately fade out. It was this version that was released as the first The The single, spending four weeks in the UK chart and reaching a high of number 68. In Australia, it fared slightly better, reaching number 43 but not quite breaching the top 40 (although it did make the top 40 in the Netherlands, reaching number 31 in its 1983 re-recorded album version). That performance was enough, though, to give both Johnson and CBS confidence.

Reviewing the single in the 30 September edition, *Smash Hits* was very positive: 'Never mind record of the week, this is the week of the The The record … [Johnson's] sleazy Lou Reed vocals contrast beautifully with the melange of smoochy synthetics, around which a delicate, folksy flute flutters from time to time.' For *Noise* magazine, Johnson's effort was 'one of the best dance records to come out of this country for a long time', with *Sounds* tagging it a 'hypnotic recording that hooks deeper into you with its casual intrusiveness the more you hear it'. *Record Mirror* was the only notable dissenter among the big music titles, declaring 'Uncertain Smile' – at just under five minutes – to be 'long and drawn out'. The delayed opening to the song and the individual elements of the instrumentation allowed for the creation of a 12" primarily intended for playing in clubs. Coming in at just under ten minutes in length (9:59), *Record Mirror* would certainly not approve, but *Zigzag* did, with Paul Barney highlighting the extended track as 'the hottest sound being played down the Camden Palace recently … ['Uncertain Smile' is] a sad, throbbing dance beat by The The. It's designed to pull at your heartstrings rather than get you moving...' The 12" was championed by club DJ Rusty Egan, who repeatedly played a pre-release version. The song's opening Xylorimba section is extended (and re-introduced halfway through), the vocals delayed with an early appearance of Cioe's flute line and the middle chant slightly elongated. What would become the extended piano solo at the end of the album version is here in draft form – alongside the saxophone central section and building rhythm track – returning again at the end of the extended release. Although consisting of only two verses and a repeated chorus, 'Uncertain Smile' built upon the progress Johnson had made in his songwriting with 'Another Boy Drowning'.

For the album version (which would become the most familiar take), the song was entirely re-recorded. Having gone through two previous iterations in 'Cold Spell Ahead' and the 7" single of 'Uncertain Smile', Johnson and new producer Hardiman were in a position to perfect their take. This final iteration was a livelier, cleaner take on the New York original (this one recorded in John Foxx's London studio, The Garden). Cripin Cioe's flute and sax contributions were dispensed with, with Andy Duncan replacing the Roland drum machine on the sticks. Where Johnson had provided the original bass guitar line, this version featured Camelle G. Hinds (both Duncan and Hinds would contribute to other *Soul Mining* tracks). Without the wind instruments, though, the final track appeared lacking. The studio boasted a Yamaha C3 baby grand piano, inspiring the musicians to wrap up the track with a lengthy piano solo. Kicking around suggestions for potential players, Jools Holland of the recently split Squeeze, and a presenter on Channel 4's music show *The Tube*, was suggested. Holland approached the job as any other session musician (he was paid £100 for 30 minutes) but was inspired by the overall track to extend what was anticipated from him even further. Johnson recalled: 'As the piano solo progressed, Hardiman and I were just looking at each other going, 'Oh, yes!' We just knew we had something special. It just built, crescendo upon crescendo. It was incredible.' Talking to *The Quietus* years later, Johnson noted of Holland, 'The last time I saw him, he said he gets asked more about that than anything else he's done'. This definitive version of 'Uncertain Smile' (re-released as a single in November 1983, but only reaching the outer edges of the chart at number 100) became a live staple on the few times that The The toured, with the three-minute piano solo at the end proving to be an epic finish, no matter who was at the keys.

'Fruit Of The Heart' 1:57 (Australia and New Zealand only)
Tacked on the end of side one of the original album, but only in the Antipodes, 'Fruit Of The Heart' provided a brief instrumental interlude before the album plunged into its second half. It's a wistful doodle, seemingly put together by Johnson solo without any additional input from his revolving set of *Soul Mining* bandmates.

'The Twilight Hour' 5:58
Charting the brutal effects of a collapsed romance, 'The Twilight Hour' is a personal cry of despair that ditches the political for the personal. It starts as the simple tale of one person waiting for a phone call from another, having decided to express their true feelings. As it goes on, it takes a darker turn, suggesting that the singer was once 'emotionally independent' but that this relationship has them 'trapped by tenderness/and beaten into submission'. The song climaxes with the ironically contradictory realisation that 'you're relying on her/for your independence'. Talking with *MOJO* in 2014, Johnson looked back upon the explicitly emotional lyrics of 'The Twilight Hour' with some

trepidation. Noting it was the 'most painful' track on *Soul Mining*, he explained: 'I wanted this sense of sweltering heat, claustrophobia, emotional paranoia. The anxiety and insecurity of a new relationship. I think I got that.' However, he regarded the emotional honesty of the lyrics as coming from a naively young mind: 'But the lyric 'Cutting chunks from your heart/and rubbing the meat into your eyes', that's really over the top. I was a kid when I wrote that.'

Playing on the track were Manyika on drums, Leer on synths and Hinds on bass, with Johnson handling the rest of the instrumentation and the vocals. An additional contribution, which made all the difference to the final track, was Martin McCarrick playing the cello. McGarrick, who also contributed to the second Marc and the Mambas album, would go on to play in Siouxsie and the Banshees between 1987 and 1995. Later, he would be part of the 4AD 'super group' This Mortal Coil and join the band Therapy?.

In *The Quietus*, Johnson recalled the emotional roots of songs like 'The Twilight Hour'. 'I went through a very lonely and introspective period, probably for about 18 months to two years … I was spending a lot of time in my bedroom with my tape recorders and going for long walks by myself … That was what I'd call an emotional hot-house experience. That period really changed me.' Johnson's unclassifiable music was labelled by John Doran as 'existential blues', and 'The Twilight Hour' is a prime example of this approach, albeit in a modern 1980s vein. Talking to *Uncut*, Johnson summed up the subject of 'The Twilight Hour' as being about 'the initial stages of the relationship. The insecurities. That awful, terrible rollercoaster ride where the walls are initially dissolving in the relationship and you're somewhere between pure euphoria and then this terrible insecurity that keeps you awake at night.'

'Soul Mining' 4:50

The album's title track appears late in the running order (second to last in Johnson's original scheme). Along with 'The Twilight Hour', 'GIANT' and 'This Is The Day', this was a song written when Johnson had reached his 20s, rather than coming from his teenage years ('Uncertain Smile', in the form of 'Cold Spell Ahead', dated to age 18, while 'Perfect' was drafted when he was 19). Like those other songs, there is an emotional maturity to 'Soul Mining' absent from some of the earlier work, especially that on *Burning Blue Soul*. Of his songwriting, Johnson told *Uncut*: 'In the early days, it's all very instinctual, just how you feel. I grew up listening to John Lennon and The Beatles. Lennon used to say, 'Tell the truth and make it rhyme.' You can't get simpler advice than that.' Opening with individual drones before the dreamy, wafting instrumentation kicks in, 'Soul Mining' initially presents as a positive sounding experience, until the lyrics tell a very different story: 'Something always goes wrong/When things are going right/You swallowed your pride/ To quell the pain inside'. In fact, emotionally it sounds like a sequel to 'The Twilight Hour': 'You've been read like an open book/Page by page/You'll never tell anyone/Your inner thoughts again'. In between this emotional angst, the break in the middle of the song is bright and moving, with Johnson handling the synths over Andy Duncan's percussion.

'GIANT' 9:36
Stylised as all caps on the album track listing, 'GIANT' embodies the collaborative approach Johnson took to putting together *Soul Mining*. He knew what he wanted his songs to sound like, and he knew he'd recruited talented musicians to help him get there. Credited as 'Frank Want', J. G. Thirlwell of Foetus fame makes his The The debut playing drums (or 'sticks', as it is credited; he built the rhythm from hitting various trays, pots and pans). Johnson had connected with Australian-born London-resident Thirlwell early in his musical journey, and they were still working together well into the 21st century. Thomas Leer was back on keyboards, while Camelle G. Hinds handled the bass guitar. Zeke Manyika was also playing drums and was instrumental in suggesting a vital component of the finished track.

By far the longest cut on *Soul Mining*, 'GIANT' was intended by Johnson to be a cinematic closer to the entire endeavour – that's why the title was all in caps (perhaps influenced by the original movie poster for the 1956 James Dean movie *Giant*). Despite all the collaborators, Johnson hand-built the track, starting with a ten-minute-long percussion click track on top of which he laid the distinctive synth line. When he got to the studio, he allocated the various parts to his collaborators. When it was all done, though, everyone felt something was still lacking. It was Manyika who suggested an African-style tribal chant. 'There was me, Matt, the engineer … Stevo was there as well', recalled Manyika in 2018. 'We did this chant, and that was it – done. Normally, when you do something, you go away and get anxious for a few days, wondering if it works. I never got that with 'GIANT'. I just knew we'd done it.' The African connection suggested by Manyika also influenced Andy Johnson's take on the cover art for *Soul Mining*, inspired by a photo of one of Fela Kuti's wives.

Before it builds to the big, percussive, chanting finish, 'GIANT' is another deep dive into Johnson's troubled psyche. 'How can anyone know me/When I don't even know myself', he asks plaintively. Before that, there are familiar themes reflected in the lyrics that have run all through this album, mainly revolving around a disintegrating sense of self: 'I am a stranger to myself'; 'When I looked into my face/It wasn't myself I'd seen/But who I tried to be'; 'I clogged up my mind/With perpetual greed'; and 'I'm caving in upon myself'. It would be a self-exploration and self-excoriation that would run through the rest of Johnson's musical output.

'Perfect' 5:36 (Single, and Australia, New Zealand, Canada and US album only)
Second single 'Perfect' (released on 11 February 1983) was originally not intended for the album, and the UK release finished with 'GIANT'. The track

was added to the American, Canadian, Australian and New Zealand releases without Johnson's authorisation. It wasn't until the 2002 remastered re-release of *Soul Mining* that he succeeded in having 'Perfect' removed from all versions of the album. As Johnson told *The Quietus*: 'Behind my back, this cheerful, avuncular guy who worked in A&R stuck 'Perfect' on the end of the album, but it was never supposed to be on there. I was livid when I found out about it. He just said, 'I thought it would be more value.' I was so angry that he would do that. I fought to get it taken off, and eventually in 2002, I got it taken off, and then I got loads of complaints from the American audiences saying, 'What the Hell has happened to the last track?' I had to explain that it wasn't supposed to be there in the first place.'

'Perfect' was the product of the second, troubled, New York recording session under the supervision of Mike Thorne. Johnson was not in a good place, feeling guilty about his recent success, and was easily led astray by his manager, Stevo Pearce. Thorne and Johnson clashed over the instruments to use on the track (which grew from an earlier effort titled 'Screw Up Your Feelings'), with Thorne proposing the Synclavier synthesiser and Johnson preferring the more compact (and cheaper) Suzuki Omnichord. Former New York Dolls singer David Johansen – brought in to provide harmonica when Johnson's quest to find 'an old blues guy' proved fruitless – was surprised by the poor atmosphere in the studio and the obvious drug-addled behaviour of Johnson and Stevo. Despite that, and Johnson's worries about his ability to authentically sing about the kind of deprivation he'd only recently avoided, the first version of 'Perfect' was laid down.

The London re-recorded version for inclusion on *Soul Mining* opens with a bold rhythm (courtesy of Andy Duncan), bass guitar (from Camelle G. Hinds), thrumming keyboards, Harry Beckett's trumpet break and Johansen's harmonica. 'Perfect' is another upbeat sounding tune (like 'Uncertain Smile') with downbeat lyrics. The perfect day of the song is ironic, from the singer's self-centred viewpoint ('Oh, what a perfect day/To think about myself'). Things take a grimmer turn when the lack of a future in early-1980s Britain is personified as a cemetery ('Passing by a cemetery/I think of all the little hopes and dreams/That lie lifeless and unfilled beneath the soil'). This culminates in the final section where the music matches the dark vision of the lyrics: 'The future is now/but it's all going wrong'. By the end, Johnson is offering a riposte to The Specials' 1981 hit 'Ghost Town' with 'This town ain't going/like a ghost town/It's going like Hell...', a yell of frustration suggesting the consumerist future planned by the Conservatives ('If you give them all your money/they'll give you their hearts') was worse than the bleak recession that The Specials had commented on. The single release certainly didn't match The Specials' number-one spot for 'Ghost Town', reaching a poor number 79 and hanging around for a mere three weeks. The original New York-recorded 12" version (8:59) featured different instrumentation and a looser, rougher vocal (Johnson sounds particularly detached and distant), but the same bleak lyrical content.

Related Tracks

Over time, as the popularity of The The and Matt Johnson grew through the 1980s, his legendary 'lost' album, *The Pornography Of Despair*, became an object of desire among fans. Johnson felt he had good reason for moving on from his unreleased second album. He told *The Quietus*, 'I was never happy with it really. It was neither one thing nor the other. It wasn't what *The Pornography Of Despair* could have been or should have been: it was a progression from *Burning Blue Soul*, but it wasn't as clean and as accomplished as *Soul Mining*.' Several of the pieces intended for that album were reworked or developed further for use on *Soul Mining* ('The Sinking Feeling', 'Uncertain Smile'), while many of the tracks were re-recorded during the *Soul Mining* sessions and ultimately pressed into service as assorted B-sides, 'bonus' tracks or extras on the UK cassette release. That allowed fans to reconstruct as best they could what Johnson had intended for *The Pornography Of Despair*. Various fan-curated bootlegs have attempted to build a running order for the unreleased album. Some followed the release order of the tracks as supporting material, while others made a 'best guess' based on the actual songs. The running order offered here is a combination of both approaches and makes no claim to being the way Johnson might have presented the material if *The Pornography Of Despair* had followed *Burning Blue Soul* (other tracks intended for the album – 'What Stanley Saw', 'Cold Spell Ahead', 'Fruit Of The Heart', 'The Sinking Feeling' and 'Perfect' – have been covered in-depth earlier).

There is still a possibility this album and the even rarer *Spirits* might yet see the light of day. Johnson has already released his first musical endeavour, *See Without Being Seen*, having realised that there was a small but keen fanbase interested in his unreleased material. Having gone through the 'baking' process that saved the original tapes of *See Without Being Seen*, Johnson may do the same again for other material. 'I'm the only person who can do it because I'm the only one who knows what to look for. That's a process that I'm looking forward to, but it's so time-consuming', he admitted to *The Quietus*. '[*The*] *Pornography Of Despair* will be fine. That will sound better than *Burning Blue Soul*. *Spirits* will sound pretty decent, but I have to make sure it sounds good and I'd like to put it out as a nice set.'

'Absolute Liberation' 4:29

Released as a bonus second 7" record packaged with the 'This Is The Day' 7" single, 'Absolute Liberation' has a deceptively gentle beginning, but is clearly tied back to the *Burning Blue Soul* era. The discursive, rambling lyric sees Johnson duet with an echoed version of himself. As more *Soul Mining*-style sounds emerge, so do similar lyrical observations: 'I'm struck dumb with mental impotence/As the feelings in my head explode in a fountain of ignorance'. The buried-in-the-mix second vocal suggests an inner voice coming from an abstract realm: 'I live in a seashell, free from the world', it says. From that vantage point, this free-floating personality is able to criticise the singer directly. The lyrics reveal the concerns and anxieties of a songwriter who was in their late teens when compiling this material: would it ever be good enough? 'You've forgotten more than you'll ever know/You only read to avoid thinking/And your head empties when you've got no one to boast to/Without the lubrication of inspiration/You're all washed up!' The production has the muddiness that permeated *Burning Blue Soul*, with hints of the same prog-psychedelia, but the clearer vocals and the guitar work also point forward to what Johnson would achieve on *Soul Mining*. An 'Absolute Liberation Part Two' appears in some listings but has never been released.

'Leap Into The Wind' 4:48

The second track featured on the bonus second 7" record packaged with the 'This Is The Day' 7" single, 'Leap Into The Wind' is introduced with synthesised woodwind sounds that are then smothered in some very distinctive guitar work later adapted for 'The Mercy Beat' on *Infected* – which shows how Johnson would never throw away a good tune or a good lyric. The lyrics and vocals are very different, however, from 'The Mercy Beat'. This is an interior narrative from a frustrated young soul, like many of Johnson's earliest songs. Lyrical ideas expressed here even carried through as far into the future as 2024's *Ensoulment*. Compare 'Leap Into The Wind' lines 'But I woke up inside a dream' to 'Life After Life's (*Ensoulment*) 'You know you're dreaming but you can't wake up'. It displays a thematic consistency across the better part of 45 years. At heart, though, 'Leap Into The Wind' is a youngster's song, concerned with frustrated romance, emotional pain and the limited horizons of a bedsit. The singer laments, 'When your lover turns out to be a figment of your imagination/Shut yourself in mind and thought and contemplation', admitting, 'I sit staring out my bedroom window/Watching the world pass me by'. The vocal is far less polished than anything on *Soul Mining*, but the personal themes are familiar.

'Dumb As Death's Head' 4:45

Intended for *The Pornography Of Despair*, 'Dumb As Death's Head' was given away as a flexi-single in a *Melody Maker* issue in 1983 (paired with The Sines' 'Jonathon') as part of the promotional drive for *Soul Mining*. The title appears to come from Sylvia Plath's *The Bell Jar*, in reference to the uselessness of a phone when you have no-one you want to call, a simile ideally suited to the kind of isolation and teen frustration that much of Johnson's early songwriting revolved around. Fresher and slightly more 'poppy' than some of the other rejected tracks, it makes sense that this was used to promote *Soul Mining*. Johnson slips into the falsetto he sometimes adopted on 'Leap Into The Wind' and the vocal is not as polished as on later work. The foregrounding of the piano flourish is a hint of things to come, though. Johnson also manages some neat lyrics that will find further life in his later work: 'This life will be the death of me'; 'My tongue is tied and my mind's eye blinded'; and 'I'm becoming trapped in a tomb of my own making'.

'Three Orange Kisses From Kazan' 4:33

The B-side to the 7" 'Uncertain Smile' single release (and one of the five extra tracks released on the UK cassette edition of *Soul Mining*), 'Three Orange Kisses From Kazan' is another *The Pornography Of Despair* reject, with its muddy production much closer to *Burning Blue Soul* than *Soul Mining* – particularly contrasted with the clear-as-a-bell A-side, 'Uncertain Smile'. Introduced with Eastern-sounding instrumentation, the song nonetheless has a percussive insistence that helps drive the vocals, delivered in an abstracted falsetto style by Johnson. The same existential concerns rise to the surface, expressed in such lines as 'I was always having trouble keeping body and soul together'; 'Why do people never say what they mean?/Why do people just repeat what they read?'; and 'I'd say our lives are not in our hands'.

In its difference from the other material on *Soul Mining* released as singles, the psychedelic 'Three Orange Kisses From Kazan' is an effective, experimental B-side. Beating 1985's *Static* (which featured the first use of 'This Is The Day'), it was 'Three Orange Kisses From Kazan' that was the first The The track licenced for film use, appearing in the 1984 film *Decoder*, alongside tracks from contemporaries like Einstürzende Neubauten, Soft Cell and Blue Rondo a la Turk. The film starred Throbbing Gristle's Genesis P-Orridge as a rebel noise-pirate high priest who discovers that replacing authoritarian state-mandated music with industrial noise changes the behaviour of a brainwashed population. This little-seen confrontational, experimental work was ideally suited as an outlet for an offbeat tune like this one.

'The Nature Of Virtue' 3:51 (Original) 5:52 (Re-recording)

Another *Pornography* track repurposed as a B-side, this time on the 'Perfect' 7" single, 'The Nature Of Virtue' is a driving cut that features classic soul-searching The The lyrics. The original, shorter recording is a mere sketch for the later re-recorded and improved track with different lyrics here and there, but the same haunting, defiant chorus line: 'Don't change yourself to suit everybody else'. The *Pornography* recording peters out, while the revised version is punchier in its delivery. Better, clearer production values and diverse instrumentation are employed to bring the draft version to new, extended life. The percussion is stronger, the musical stings more effective, the piano stronger and the vocals head-and-shoulders above the original, more meandering take.

Lyrically, Johnson expands his repertoire while staying true to his concerns: 'You lay staring at your ceiling through all of the night/And out to haunt you come the ghosts of your life'. Examining the title subject, Johnson explores the questions every teen asks themselves on the verge of responsible adulthood: 'You can't admit, but you can't deny/A small heart, a spiteful mind/Are you good or bad you ask yourself/And do the things you do hurt the ones who care the most for you?' The revised version is strong enough to have found a place among the other tracks on *Soul Mining*, and in re-recording it, Johnson must have recognised this. Pressed into use as a B-side, however, it still found an audience.

'Mental Healing Progress (For A Mixed Up Kid)' 3:45
Given its sound and instrumentation, as well as lyrical preoccupations, 'Mental Healing Process' was an ideal B-side for the 7" single release of 'This Is The Day'. It begins as more bedsit worries about the passing of time and the lack of personal achievement, pumped up by the insistent, darker chorus: 'Keep on making those pointless decisions everyday/You'll be in another world tonight anyway'. The song switches back and forward between the two modes, the personal ruminations on pain (presented against light and upbeat music) and the scolding chorus (against a much darker musical environment). It was a song structure that Matt Johnson would get much mileage from.

'Waitin' For The Upturn' 4:30
Released as the B-side to the 12" 'Uncertain Smile' single, and paired with 'Three Orange Kisses From Kazan', 'Waitin' For The Upturn' was once considered for possible single release in its own right. Echoing the 'Mental Healing Process' line 'All's not well with yourself', 'Waitin' For The Upturn' offers: 'Do you live alone, do you try to hide/That something's not quite right inside of you?' Musically, this occasionally sounds like something from *Breaking Glass*-era Hazel O'Connor (specifically the sax on 'Will You?', oddly). Supported by some sharp guitar work, 'Waitin' For The Upturn' is an effective early-1980s teen anthem that engages with alienation ('Standing under a tree in the pouring rain/Smoking someone else's last cigarette, again') and even nuclear war anxiety ('I'm gonna build up stocks for the end of civilisation').

'Soup Of Mixed Emotions' 3:17
An indication of Matt Johnson's future direction when it came to scoring films, the instrumental 'Soup Of Mixed Emotions' is an atmospheric piece that saw the light of day on an unofficial 1983 The The compilation titled *Early Rarities*. Dominated by percussion, Johnson moves through various instruments with some of the sounds recalling effects heard on other The The tracks of this period. A minute before the end, it morphs into something that sounds like an off-cut from 'Three Orange Kisses From Kazan', but just not so 'eastern'.

Infected (1986)

Personnel:
Matt Johnson: guitar, keyboards, percussion, vocals
David Palmer: drums
Luis Jardim: percussion
Warne Livesey: bass, organ, backing vocals, string arrangements
Neneh Cherry: vocals on 'Slow Train To Dawn'
Dan K. Brown: electric bass
Jeff Clyne: acoustic bass
Dave Clayton: synth bass
Steve Hogarth: piano
Gary Moberley: Fairlight CMI synth
Bashiri Johnson: percussion
Roli Mosimann: percussion, programming
Bob Mintzer, Jamie Talbot: saxophones
Andrew Blake: baritone saxophone
Guy Baker: trumpet, flugelhorn
John 'J. G.' Thirlwell, David Defries, John Edcott: trumpet
Pete Beachill, Ashley Slater, Steve Aitken: trombones
Philip Eastop: French horn
Judd Lander: harmonica
Tessa Niles, Zeke Manyika, Anna Domino, the Croquets: backing vocals
The Astari String Orchestra: strings
Gavin Wright: orchestra leader
The Deaf Section: brass
Anne Dudley, Andrew Poppy: brass arrangements
Recorded at The Garden, Air, and Livingston Studios (London); mixed at Comforts Place, Sussex, between 1985 and 1986
Producers: Warne Livesey, Matt Johnson, Roli Mosimann, Gary Langan
Label: Some Bizzare (UK)/Epic (US)
Release date: 17 November 1986 (UK)
Charts: UK: 14, Aus: 15, Netherlands: 46, New Zealand: 12, Norway: 14, Sweden: 20
Running time: 40:57
All tracks written by Matt Johnson, except where noted

With *Soul Mining*, Matt Johnson had created his ideal band format – one in which he'd be the only permanent member. The The would function as an ever-changing roster of guest musicians, producers and collaborators, all working under the guidance of Johnson. It was a set-up that worked well, allowing him to control the work but also to bring in inspirations and contributions from others. Johnson noted: 'The The was ... constantly changing – I was never quite sure who was in and who was out', later adding, 'the people I would like to play with always have other commitments.' Nevertheless, his band of misfits had made enough of an impact for the *NME* to name Johnson joint ninth 'Best New Act' of 1983 in tandem with Paul Young.

Although *Soul Mining* had not been a massive hit – released in October 1983, it had spent three weeks in the UK top 40 Album Chart, peaking at number 27 – it had proved to be an effective calling card. Johnson was now a presence on the British music scene, even if he'd failed to make any significant impact on the Singles Chart. The process of creating *Soul Mining* – 'having to do so much so fast', as Johnson put it – had exhausted him. Hospital checks failed to turn up anything concerning. During the press tour promoting *Soul Mining*, Johnson was optimistic about following up with new work in short order, telling *Juke* magazine a new album and supporting videos would soon follow, along with another single titled 'Body Work' (ultimately not to appear). He promised 'a total departure, musically and lyrically'. There then followed over a year's silence...

During his absence in 1984, Johnson was building his own recording studio while starting to write the material that would ultimately make up *Infected* (1986). CBS wanted a new album from The The in 1984, but that would mean recording that summer, which Johnson was not ready to commit to. As Some Bizzare's Stevo put it, Johnson would record 'when he feels inspired or when he feels the time is right ... we record when, where and how we want'. The dispute that resulted saw CBS offer to terminate Johnson's contract for $60,000 – a sum Stevo attempted to raise from other record companies, only for CBS to withdraw the offer. It was the kind of interference guaranteed to ensure Johnson delayed further and put any idea of a tour supporting *Soul Mining* far from his mind.

Rather than building on *Soul Mining*'s momentum, it would be three years before he offered a follow-up. Although Johnson was only aged 22-23, he had actually produced several albums of material, using up his reservoir of songs. 'You've got to take time to fill up on experiences again', noted Johnson. 'I became more and more interested in politics and religious affairs ... trying to look outside of my own tiny orbit.' Johnson took every chance offered by Stevo to escape that 'tiny orbit' with the pair regularly flying off on exotic jaunts, taking in America, Italy, Egypt and Mombasa in Kenya, some of which would feed into *Infected*.

Johnson felt the UK Conservative government was 'forcing people who wouldn't normally be political to become more political', as he told interviewer Andy Dunkley in December 1986. The Falklands War of 1982, the American bombing of Libya in 1986 and the general dilapidated state of the United Kingdom in the early to mid 1980s under the Conservatives would find an outlet in songs like 'Heartland', 'Angels Of Deception' and 'Sweet Bird Of Truth'.

Looking for a grittier sound to match this subject matter – while still including songs on 'love, sex, and death' like 'Out Of The Blue (Into The Fire)' and 'Slow Train To Dawn' – Johnson immersed himself in the blues. Johnson was inspired by movies as much as by music, contributing to an epic, widescreen sound in story-driven tracks like 'Twilight Of A Champion' and 'The Mercy Beat'. All this would culminate in *Infected: The Movie*.

While developing *Infected* during 1985, Johnson met Warne Livesey, a producer working in London, during a meeting set up by J. G. Thirlwell. Livesey had previously worked with The Specials, Coil, Thirlwell's Foetus and Thomas Dolby. He was keen to work with Johnson, impressed with the high quality of his demos, while Johnson was looking to import a harder-edged, cleaner sound than that achieved previously. Livesey was soon on board to produce *Infected*, impressed by the expenditure CBS lavished on the project: 'There was never really a budget. We just got what we needed. It was close to $300,000 we spent, but that's a guess. We spent nearly a year in the studio, on and off...' The money invested in *Infected* suggested CBS were not too worried about Johnson's tendency to work at his own, often languorous, pace – as long as he produced the goods.

Infected was met with largely positive reviews. As the long-awaited follow-up to *Soul Mining*, *Melody Maker* declared *Infected* to be 'a one-man vision of terrifying proportions.' For *Record Mirror*, 'two sides of this intense brooding can be a bit much to take, and the lyrics are at times self-consciously poetic. *Infected* might not be particularly optimistic, but it is rather good.' *Q* regarded Johnson's efforts as 'grim stuff, with the lyrical tension well-matched by the music', describing the result as 'a bizarre collision between Soft Cell and Tom Waits.' For *Sounds*, there was 'self-controlled passion and strength seeping out all over this thing.' A dissenting opinion came from *NME*'s Danny Kelly, who regarded *Infected* as 'shocking' before asking 'what remains after the shock wears off? The answer will vary, naturally, from one burning blue soul to the next; for me, the lasting afterglow is one of detachment ... In the final analysis, living with *Infected* ... you'll be impressed, sure, but you won't grow to love it.' Despite that opinion, the darker songs and more aggressive music of *Infected* proved appealing to Britain's record buyers. *Infected* spent 30 weeks on the UK Album Chart, with seven of those weeks in the top 40, hitting a peak of number 14. The single 'Heartland' gave Johnson his biggest hit yet, reaching number 29 and spending 11 weeks in the chart.

There was much more to the *Infected* project than just the album. Johnson conceived of an audacious marketing gambit. In 1986, he explained his reasoning to *NME*'s Ian Pye: 'I came to a crossroads in my career, really. Having not played live for three and a half years and having such a low profile – for instance, not having my picture on my sleeves – I decided to raise the whole stakes and risk becoming known a lot more as a personality, not really something I'm keen on.' It was a decision that would have profound consequences.

Johnson's notion was to create a music video for each of the eight tracks on *Infected* that, when strung together, would make up a complete visual interpretation. The completed film was intended as a replacement for a world tour, something Johnson was reluctant to undertake. Ever the entrepreneur, Johnson's manager, Stevo Pearce, managed to persuade a reluctant CBS to finance the project to the tune of £350,000 (over and above the cost of the studio recording of *Infected*).

The first video was for 'Heartland', shot at Greenwich Power Station by director Peter Christopherson (known as 'Sleazy', he was part of the Some Bizzare wider family and a founding member of Throbbing Gristle). Mark Romanek, the director of *Static* (1985), was recruited for 'Sweet Bird Of Truth'. Romanek would go on to make more pop videos for artists such as Nine Inch Nails and David Bowie, among many others.

Johnson, along with Stevo, Christopherson and producer Aubrey Powell, set out for the jungles of South America to shoot videos for 'Infected' and 'The Mercy Beat'. Settling in Iquitos, Bolivia (only accessible by boat or plane), Johnson hired a local Indian tribe to serve as guides. They showed the filmmakers the jungle while also introducing them to local hallucinogens, which Johnson proved enthusiastic to sample. Things spiralled from there.

On a 'making of' documentary for *Infected: The Movie*, Johnson explained how he became caught up in the exoticism of South America. 'You can sense the spirits in the air, there is something magical about the place. The heat started getting to people, and also people were doing things they shouldn't have done, I suppose. I'm not excluding myself from blame, but you get carried away, and everyone got up to things that you can't really talk about.' The filming of 'The Mercy Beat', amid a band of local communist rebels, was the climax of a fraught time, few details of which those involved could accurately recall. Johnson remembers being 'so high' much of the time.

After a month in the jungle, the team arrived in New York to shoot 'Out Of The Blue (Into The Fire)' in Spanish Harlem. Matching the song's narrative, filming took place in a brothel next door to a crack house. A drunk Johnson exacerbated a tense situation when he threw a bottle at a gang of drug dealers. Tim Pope directed both that and the video for 'Twilight Of A Champion', which saw Johnson put a real loaded gun in his mouth. 'I wanted to see what it felt like', he explained to *Melody Maker* in 1986. 'To have all that power, to be so close to dying. It's incredible.' According to Pope, Johnson was 'very difficult, dangerous even ... he was really edgy ... very difficult to work with.' Despite the tensions, Johnson still declares the video for 'Out Of The Blue (Into The Fire)' to be his all-time favourite.

Back in Britain, the project was completed with the final videos for 'Angels Of Deception' (directed by Alastair McIlwain) and 'Slow Train To Dawn' (directed by Tim Pope), which featured an appearance by Neneh Cherry, who'd duetted with Johnson on the album cut. The video, a pastiche of silent movies like *The Perils Of Pauline* (1914), saw Cherry tied to the railway tracks while Johnson drives a train heading for her.

Infected: The Movie premiered at Notting Hill's Electric Cinema and was broadcast by Channel 4 on 16 December 1986, followed by a screening on MTV. Released to cinemas worldwide, the 47-minute film was also released on VHS (but never on DVD). It was later screened (alongside *The Inertia Variations*, 2017) at the 2017 Edinburgh International Film Festival in a retrospective.

As with *Soul Mining*, Johnson paid the price for giving his all to the *Infected* project. The drink and the drugs took a toll on his health, his relationship with Fiona Skinner collapsed and he withdrew from making music to focus on recovering his mental and physical health. Johnson discovered that he and fame did not really mix. In 2002, he told *MOJO* magazine: 'I took a long, hard look at myself and realised I didn't like the way I was acting ... That initial flush of success is a toxin; it really warps people's personalities for the worse and I didn't like what it did to me.'

'Infected' 4:49

The album's title track was the second single issued (on 13 October 1986), breaching the top 50, reaching number 48. It was evident that this was a much harder-edged sound than anything on *Soul Mining*. At the height of the AIDS epidemic, Johnson proposed love as a disease with opening line 'Infect me with your love'. The layers of percussion (Dave Palmer on drums, accompanied by sampled kick drums) and the insistent guitar line (real guitars – Dan Brown's electric bass – and sampled guitars) project a muscular sound, over which Guy Barker's trumpet intrudes. It's well over a minute before Johnson's main vocals begin, a first-person account of being driven mad with lust and desire. The chorus – 'I can't give you up till I've/Got more than enough/So infect me with your love' – outlines the male greed for sex, followed by the suggestion of love-as-illness: 'Nurse me into sickness/Nurse me back to health' and then 'When desire becomes an illness/Instead of a joy/And guilt a necessity/That's gotta be destroyed'. Tessa Niles' backing vocals run throughout (accompanied by percussionist Zeke Manyika), taking over towards the fade out. It's a frenetic song that doesn't stop for breath, full of energy. The urgency of 'Infected' was a huge contrast to the songs on *Soul Mining*. Teen angst was replaced by the lust, desire and aggression of a 20-something male voice making its mark on the world.

The music video – the opening section of *Infected: The Movie* – runs a slightly longer 5:02. In it, Johnson is strapped into a chair atop a boat cruising up an African river, intercut with images of local life, shot in La Paz, Bolivia. From behind sunglasses and a bandana, he delivers the vocals while his chair is taken from the boat and carried through town. Behind Johnson's head, the background locations change before he's then seen in a hospital environment. The video concludes with Johnson treated as a sacrificial victim, burned before an enthusiastic audience, before reappearing in the crowd puffing on a cigarette under a Coca-Cola emblazoned baseball cap. Although the song is about love and sex, Johnson intended to get across the idea of the West 'infecting' the Third World with its capitalistic vices (hence Coca-Cola).

Johnson worked with his brother, Andrew 'Andy Dog' Johnson, to provide the distinctive illustrative material for the entire *Infected* project. Of the controversial image on the single packaging for 'Infected', Johnson noted: 'The masturbating devil was something [Andy] had already done ... There was outrage, but we couldn't stop laughing about it ... Probably it was a bit childish, but we used to get a kick out of shocking people back then.' The original art was withdrawn from sale and replaced with something less controversial – a severely cropped version of the original.

'Out Of The Blue (Into The Fire)' 5:10
The sleazy seeds planted by 'Infected' reached full bloom in 'Out Of The Blue (Into The Fire)'. It's a straightforward narrative of a dissatisfied character's empty encounter with a prostitute ('I'm a man without a soul/I lost it while parading it/In a town full of thieves'). It plays with identity: in preparation, the narrator adopts an alternative personality ('I thought if I acted like someone else/I'd feel more comfortable with myself'). The account gets more graphic and may have been drawn from Johnson's own life as an on-the-rise 20-something. Accompanying the lyrics is a dynamic and dramatic musical construction, with the drums driving the aggression of a song about selfish sexual release ('Don't tell me what your name is/I want your body, not your mind/I want a feeling worth paying for before I say goodbye').

The bass (acoustic: Jeff Cline, electric: Dan Brown) powers the track, with judicious wind instruments (flugelhorn: Guy Baker, trombone: Pete Beachill) adding emotion. It is, however, the use of live strings (the Astari String Orchestra) and female backing vocals (Tessa Niles again) that really makes 'Out Of The Blue (Into The Fire)' something special. Johnson and Livesey argued with CBS to secure the extra funding for the strings, used here and on 'Heartland'. Together, they bring some humanity to the cold-hearted encounter the lyrics depict, adding to the emotional unravelling of the song's subject ('I was trying so hard to be myself/I was turning into somebody else'). The strings bring a grace note to an otherwise cold tale about the emptiness of sex without love.

The accompanying video was (as the filming on location in New York's Bowery might suggest) a fairly literal take on the song's story. Leaving his room and driving into the night, Johnson is joined in his open-top car by a seemingly imaginary woman sitting astride him, an encapsulation of his frustration. Arriving at the brothel ('hotel'), he's split in two – the original Johnson, in jeans and white T-shirt, never crosses the threshold of the room, while his alter-ego (sans T-shirt) is pulled in by the woman inside. She's given the final Niles-sung vocal part, while the original Johnson turns away from the scene. 'Infected' and 'Out Of The Blue (Into The Fire)' made for a challenging pair of opening tracks, immediately revealing that this album was certainly not going to be *Soul Mining* part two.

'Heartland' 5:01

The first single released (on 4 August 1986) from 'Infected' became the album's most widely-heard track and Johnson's biggest hit to date (a slow seven-week climb to number 29, spending 11 weeks on the chart, five of them in the top 40). A boldly political attack on the Conservative government of 1980s Britain, Johnson long-rated 'Heartland' as 'probably the best song I've ever written'. He told *NME* in 1986 that putting the song together had taken him the better part of 18 months, a process of refining the lyrics and matching them with suitable music.

It's a state of the nation account, chronicling the crumbling infrastructure and under-investment in services ('Past the Saturday morning cinema/That lies crumbling to the ground/And the piss stinking shopping centre/In the new side of town'). The 'piss stinking' line saw 'Heartland' briefly banned by Radio 1 until a suitably sanitised 'radio edit' was created. Johnson carefully honed his lyrics, drawing upon recent news stories about the state of Britain, in its physical infrastructure, morally and socially ('This is the land, where nothing changes/The land of red buses and blue-blooded babies/This is the place where pensioners are raped/And the heart's being cut from the welfare state'). The rising anger, seen through industrial action and protest movements, is an inevitable result ('Well it ain't written in the papers, but it's written on the walls/The way this country is divided to fall'). The American-driven wars, fuelled by patriotism and religion, get a mention, as do Britain's own military adventures in the Falklands – all intended as profit centres and distraction for the cowed populace ('The ammunition's being passed/And the lord's been praised/But the wars on the televisions/Will never be explained'). Those who benefit are clear, and it's not the people but those who participated in the deregulation 'big bang' in the City of London ('All the bankers gettin' sweaty/Beneath their white collars/As the pound in our pocket/Turns into a dollar'). The final refrain, both a warning and a lament, repeats until the fade: 'This is the 51st state of the USA'.

A strong piano line (Steve Hogarth) in the first half, and an equally strong harmonica performance (Judd Lander) provide an uplifting musicality that doesn't match the downbeat lyrics. The live Astari String Orchestra (arranged by Johnson and Livesey, led by Gavin Wright) give emotional heft, while Tessa Niles' backing vocals provide some soul.

The accompanying video is built around a performance by Johnson in front of a giant video screen (depicting images of contemporary 1980s Britain) to an audience of one, a Coke-guzzling teen girl. Almost as much as 'This Is The Day', 'Heartland' would be a trademark The The track, one as relevant in Starmer's Britain as it was in Thatcher's. Of 'Heartland', Johnson said (in *Record Mirror*): 'It sums up everything I'm saying ... It sums up my feelings for this country, which although it frequently disgusts me, I still feel for it.'

'Angels Of Deception' 4:37

Closing side one, 'Angels Of Deception' is another narrative-driven track, engaging directly with the 'great Satan' (in the words of Iran's Ayatollah Khomeini, a phrase coined during the 1979 US/Iran hostage crisis): America. The rise of neoliberal right-wing economic theory was behind both the Prime Ministership of Margaret Thatcher and the Presidency of Ronald Reagan (both worked together, building upon the so-called post-war 'special relationship'). Definitions vary, but 'neoliberalism' primarily describes market-driven capitalistic reforms of an economy and society to control markets to keep a sated population in line while still producing huge financial and status benefits for those at the top of the economic chain. The ideas dated as far back as the 1930s, but really came into prominence in the 1980s and would more or less dominate Western economic thought well into the 21st century.

Johnson wrote 'Angels Of Deception' (and 'Heartland') from the frontlines of the economic and social results of neoliberalism, focusing on American imagery filtered through a British perspective ('Well, it's high noon at the UK corral'). Neoliberalism sought to placate populations through consumer goods and cheap housing ('Well, what's a man go left to fight for/When he's bought his freedom') while setting neighbours against one another in a competition for resources in order to 'keep up with the Joneses' ('Come on down, the Devil's in town/He's brought you sticks and stones/To bust your neighbours bones'). Johnson includes a direct reference to the biggest UK-US co-operation – the siting of American Cruise missile nuclear weapons on British soil and the full-throated pursuit of neoliberal economic theory ('He's stuck his missiles in your gardens/And his theories down your throat'). The Devil/He referred to in the lyrics is clearly Khomeini's 'great Satan', America itself personified in the figure of Reagan. Again, the female chorus and backing vocals (provided by The Croquets) bring some heart to the cynical lyrics. The video depicts Johnson as a face-painted 'Andy Dog illustration come to life, amid desert and urban American landscapes represented through model work and animation.

'Sweet Bird Of Truth' 5:22

The fourth and final single released from *Infected* was 'Sweet Bird Of Truth' (released on 11 May 1987, it reached number 55), produced by Swiss-born Roli Mosimann. Another epic, cinematic, narrative-driven song, 'Sweet Bird Of Truth' chronicles the last moments of an American USAF pilot whose plane has run into trouble over the Gulf of Arabia. Opening with some military radio chatter ('Your first target is a blockhouse. Target number 11 at the North East corner of the combat zone. Request napalm.'; an opening missing from the video version), followed by chants of 'Arabia', the track unfolds the growing battle between the West and Islam, as relevant in the 21st century as it was in the 1980s.

Stately percussion (from Mosimann, along with Bashiri Johnson) forms the backdrop to the vocals from Johnson, with Anna Domino supplying a much-needed female counterpoint with her accompaniment (fittingly, Domino – actually Anna Delroy – was born in a US military hospital in Tokyo, Japan in 1955 as her father was a private in the US Army). A late-emerging saxophone (Bob Mintzer) adds to the stew.

Originally intended as the album's initial single release, the dates coincided with the April 1986 US bombing of Libya. The critique of American militarism made CBS uneasy, so the release was put back and was eventually only put out as an immediately deleted 12". The *NME* labelled 'Sweet Bird Of Truth' as 'the Single of the Year (so far)', while *Record Mirror* condemned it as 'rather ponderous and drawn out.' Mark Romanek's video depicts a war-torn wasteland through which Johnson wanders as the song's pilot, and represents Domino's vocals as coming from a skull-clutching angelic figure.

'Slow Train To Dawn' 4:14

While many of the songs on *Infected* were strongly political, drawing on contemporary events, they never entirely excluded the personal. Each song included lines that positioned Johnson's narrator as either emotionally conflicted ('My heart is heavy/My head is confused/And my aching little soul/Has started burning blue!' – 'Infected'), lost and alone ('Yeah I was feeling strong mouthed and weak willed/When I ran into the cure for my ills' – 'Out Of The Blue (Into The Fire)') or scared of the future ('Cos deep in the heart of me/There's a frightened man breaking out' – 'Angels Of Deception'). In 'Sweet Bird Of Truth', he'd been a mere man, crumbling in the face of war: 'Time was when I seemed to know/Just like any other G.I. Joe/Should I cry like a baby, or die like a man/While the planet's little wars start joining hands'.

For the third single, 'Slow Train To Dawn' (released on 12 January 1987, spending three weeks in the UK Singles Chart, hitting a high of number 64), Johnson focused exclusively upon a disintegrating personal relationship. Effectively a duet with Neneh Cherry (the Swedish-born stepdaughter of jazz musician Don Cherry; her appearance on 'Slow Train To Dawn' predated her chart success with 1989's number-three chart hit 'Buffalo Stance'), the song alternates viewpoints between a man and a woman whose life together is slowly unravelling. Headlined by saxophone from Jamie Talbot and top-line trumpet from J. G. Thirlwell, the track chugs forward over a sinister synth bassline from Dave Clayton. It features the first (but not the last) appearance of the lyric: 'I'm just another Western guy/With desires that I can't satisfy'. Talking to 'Betty Page' (Beverly Glick) in *Record Mirror*, Johnson confessed: "Slow Train To Dawn' is about the psychological relationship between two people and the weakness of the male in that relationship, and infidelity, which is borne from insecurity and weakness. It was a difficult song to write. It's my girlfriend's [Fiona Watson] favourite song now. She understands me and lets me get away with a lot, I suppose...' Johnson's experiences away from Watson heavily contributed to their slow breakup in the wake of the entire *Infected* project, but her influence on The The lives on to this day in the distinctive and unique typography she devised for the band's logo.

'Twilight Of A Champion' 4:22

Both 'Twilight Of A Champion' and closing track 'The Mercy Beat' are of a piece – strong narrative tracks that feature trade-offs in life (literally in the second case in a deal with the Devil). Johnson wrote the lyrics but co-composed the music with producer Roli Mosimann. Over the sounds of the city, a trumpet blasts and tinkling percussion sneaks in as Johnson delivers his spoken word opening. Machine gun percussion follows as punctuation. Heavily driven by brass instruments arranged by composer Andrew Poppy and featuring Andy Blake on baritone saxophone, Philip Eastop on French Horn, Ashley Slater and Steve Aitken on trombone, and Dave de Fries and John Edcott on trumpet, it's a pre-echo of the approach Johnson would take to his next album, 1989's *Mind Bomb*.

The song deconstructs the corporations and the people who run them in both Britain and America: 'A big shot, overlooking this black iron skyline/ Surrounded by his symbols of prosperity/Sits back in his new leather chair/ Ripped off the back of some unfortunate beast'. The corporate giants are supported (literally held up) by the work of others, who see in their overlords their own possible future as, according to Johnson, 'Anybody can be a millionaire/So everybody's gotta try/But by the laws of this human jungle/ Only the heartless will survive'. The inspiration for the entire *Infected* project even gets a look-in, as Johnson catalogues the travels (often with Some Bizzare's own Devil, Stevo) that helped open his eyes to worldwide inequality and exploitation by the West of the Third World: 'From Mombasa to Miami, Beirut to Bangladesh/I've flown around the world standing/On the wing of a jet'. Behind all this is a search for the safety and certainty of blissful childhood, a state-of-mind impossible to recapture in the adult world: 'Searchin' for the world I left behind/A shadow hunting shadows of childhood life/It's all I want and all I miss/But how can I return, to a place that don't exist!'. Johnson's battle between the safety and security of childhood and the dog-eat-dog corporate world of the 'loadsamoney' 1980s ends in a dark place, as suicide is suggested: 'Oh, the hand that wrote the agony/Has just begun/Will be the hand that pulls the trigger/Of this gun!'.

It was a moment depicted literally in the accompanying New York-set video during which a young lad finds a discarded gun in a burnt-out car in an industrial wasteland. The linking of that with the depiction of a corporate big shot blowing their brains out prefigures events like the disappearance of corrupt businessman Robert Maxwell in 1991 and any number of corporate scandals leading to the economic crash of 2008. This all goes hand-in-hand with the spate of American school shootings, but also the closer-to-home Dunblane massacre of Primary school children in 1996. The linking of corporate greed with the too-easily-accepted needless deaths of children by violence can be read into 'Twilight Of A Champion'.

'The Mercy Beat' 7:22

Johnson's cinematic storytelling reaches its apotheosis with the epic 'The Mercy Beat', a song that describes the consequences from the deal with the Devil that hangs over much of *Infected*, with references to Hell and Heaven in 'Heartland', 'Angels Of Deception' and 'Sweet Bird Of Truth' ('Heaven sent/ And Hell bent'), and the Devil directly in 'Angels Of Deception' and 'Twilight Of A Champion' ('Y'see, I've sold my soul/To pay for my dinner'). This Luciferian pact comes to fruition in 'The Mercy Beat' ('So one day, I asked the angels for inspiration/But the Devil bought me a drink/And he's been buying them ever since'). The song was a response to an episode in Johnson's real life, a drug-induced incident that he felt challenged his sanity in New York: 'The song was based on a knife fight with the Devil. I was scared then; I thought I was actually going to kill myself. I felt this overwhelming urge to jump off buildings, which was terrifying.'

Against backing vocals from The Croquets and brass from The Deaf Section, Johnson outlines his adventures on the wild side. Here again, he's 'just another Western guy/With desires that couldn't be satisfied', so he asked Satan to satisfy them instead. The insistent brass provides a heartbeat rhythm ('Tonight my heart's not thumping/A mercy beat') against the all-pervading drums. Trying to pull one over on Lucifer ('Y'see he tricked me into temptation/So I've tricked him into this confrontation'), the narrator plans to 'have little Lucifer, runnin' off to purgatory/With his tail between his legs/I'm gonna teach him a lesson/He ain't ever gonna forget'. Buried inside this tale of a titanic battle is also a commentary on songwriting itself: 'I never said I was the man I appeared to be/ Not the flesh wrapped around the bones of necessity/Or the soul on fire/ Scribbling thoughts for posterity'. The final video in *Infected: The Movie*, 'The Mercy Beat' sees Johnson driving through Bolivia picking up a diminutive top-hatted Devil figure and a Christian priest, intercut with elements from the previous videos in a not-entirely-successful attempt to unify the themes of the album. There's another appearance by Coca-Cola, though – this time on a poster.

Related Tracks
'Disturbed' 2:24

Released as the B-side to the 7" 'Infected' single, 'Disturbed' is another percussion-driven instrumental track in keeping with much of *Infected*, although seemingly influenced by the then-emerging New York hip hop and scratching scene. It powers along with what sounds like human moans, but is probably a sampled or electronically generated sound. More 'found sounds', like a motor engine (again created electronically) and a final rhythm part that harkens back to *Burning Blue Soul*'s opening track 'Red Cinders In The Sand', wrap things up nicely.

'Harbour Lights' 3:37

Billed as one of two *Themes From The Nightwatchman* (the other being 'Sleeping Juice'), 'Harbour Lights' was released as the B-side to the single releases of both 'Sweet Bird Of Truth' (released only as an 8:40 12"; it also featured 'Sleeping Juice' on the B-side) and 'Slow Train To Dawn'. Opening with some squeeze box, this is a high-pitched piece of possible film music, showing that Johnson was dabbling in the field as early as the mid-1980s. It's an evocative piece anticipating some of his later work on *Dusk* and *Naked Self*.

'Sleeping Juice' 2:42

The second of the *Themes From The Nightwatchman*, 'Sleeping Juice' was issued as the additional B-side track on the 12" 'Sweet Bird Of Truth'. Another atmosphere piece, it seems initially ponderous, until a light flute emerges at about 45 seconds, adding some life to the relentless, slow rhythm. A slight keyboard synth line also appears, as the track builds but never really reaches a crescendo. Presumably intended as background film music, or an experiment in that direction, Johnson felt these pieces were complete enough to be released as inconsequential B-sides.

'Flesh And Bones' 4:00

More substantial was 'Flesh And Bones', issued as a single-sided promo single in 1985 (with a second release backed by 'Waiting To Fall' by Virginia Astley, another Some Bizzare artist) and included on second Some Bizzare compilation album, 1985's *If You Can't Please Yourself, You Can't Please Your Soul* (a very Matt Johnson lyric line), produced by Paul Hardiman. Very electronic, 'Flesh And Bones' derives from Johnson's bedsitter period, recalling much of *Burning Blue Soul* and even *Soul Mining*. Interestingly, it contains the line 'The cranes are moving on the skyline', later used on 'Heartland' (to which this track also saw release as the B-side). The personal content that opens the song (another getting up out of bed start) gives way to more political concerns that would be better developed on *Soul Mining* through to *Infected* and *Mind Bomb*. Especially notable are the very-1980s, yet utterly timeless lines:

> The hypocrites on the television screens
> Are trying to disguise what they really mean
> They say things are gettin' better
> When we know they gettin' worse
> While they're buying bigger guns
> From a shrinking purse

'Born In The New S.A.' 1:58

The brief 'Born In The New S.A.' also featured (alongside 'Flesh And Bones') on the B-side to 'Heartland'. Against a gently ticking rhythm track and drums from Zeke Manyika, some media quotes from South African foreign minister P. W. Botha (or white supremacist Eugène Terre'Blanche, sources differ) play out, including the comments 'Blacks can never change their identity', 'You cannot buy civilisation' and 'I'm not a racist'. It's an obvious critique of the contradictory views of those who ran apartheid South Africa, soon to be swept away by the tide of history despite overt support from then British Prime Minister (and Matt Johnson hate figure) Margaret Thatcher. Further lines from 'Flesh And Bone' might have suited what the white hegemony were facing: 'These times they are a-changing/But I'm being left behind'.

Mind Bomb (1989)

Personnel:
Matt Johnson: vocals, guitar, keyboards
Johnny Marr: guitar, harmonica
James Eller: bass guitar
David Palmer: drums
Sinéad O'Connor: vocals on 'Kingdom Of Rain'
'Wix' (Paul Wickens): piano, keyboards, Hammond organ, accordion
Warne Livesey: keyboards, banjo, acoustic guitar
Pandit Dinesh, Danny Cummings, Pedro Haldermann: percussion
Chris White, Philip Todd: saxophone
Ashley Slater: trombone
John Eacott: flugelhorn
Mark Feltham: harmonica
Danny Thompson: upright bass on 'August & September'
Sarah Homer: clarinet
Dai Pritchard: bass clarinet
Hilary Storer: oboe
Gavyn Wright: Arabian fiddle
Astari String Section: strings
Recorded at The Garden, London; Wessex Sound Studios, London; Livingston Studios, London; Air Studios, London, between summer 1988 and May 1989
Producers: Warne Livesey, Matt Johnson, Roli Mosimann
Label: Some Bizzare (UK)/Epic (US)
Release date: 15 May 1989 (UK)/11 July 1989 (US)
Charts: UK: 4, US: 138, Aus: 32, Netherlands: 39, Germany: 24, New Zealand: 3, Sweden: 30
Running time: 45:59
All tracks written by Matt Johnson, except where noted

Matt Johnson seemed with *Infected* to have cracked the code of how to promote music without going on a gruelling world tour. The The was not a band, as such – it was an ever-changing lineup of creative contributors who worked under the direction of Johnson. Reproducing something as intricately constructed as *Infected* in the live arena was daunting, even more so for an artist who was then reluctant to tour. CBS, however, demanded he participate in the promotion of his own work. The *Infected* film project was one way Johnson had of communicating his music to a far wider audience than he might have reached on tour, while his promotional interview commitments saw him spend the better part of a year – on and off – taking part in hundreds of individual interviews. 'It's not natural to spend six months talking about yourself', Johnson lamented to Melbourne's *The Daily News*. 'You start to get selfish and self-obsessed. Everything gets very cloudy; you end up talking about your ideas and philosophies so much that they end up being worn out.'

One thing Matt Johnson certainly was at the end of the *Infected* project, including the promotion, was 'worn out'. Focused on promoting the record, Johnson wasn't writing new material and he wasn't benefiting from being around other creative collaborators. He was also depressed by the state of the UK in the late 1980s, as was evident from much of the material on *Infected*, especially 'Heartland'. The success of *Infected* was almost as big a problem for Johnson as anything else – the more it sold, the more CBS required him to promote it.

The answer to his deepening despair about the state of Britain seemed to lie in America, in particular New York, where he was increasingly spending more time. He'd throw himself into the New York nightlife and sample the opportunities of living in America for brief periods, only to return home to disappointment. 'It was a period of extreme hedonism and narcissism', was how Johnson described the second half of the 1980s to his biographer Neil Fraser. '[It] felt like being sat at the top of a world gone mad. As a contrast, I would arrive back at our flat in grey and drizzly Stoke Newington and start to feel a bit claustrophobic.'

While Johnson had been working on and promoting *Infected*, the music of the 1980s had changed. Long gone was the innovation of the early decade, with post-punk and the New Romantic movements fading as electronic instruments (once a defining feature) became incorporated into the mainstream. The best-selling singles of 1985 included songs from Jennifer Rush, Elaine Paige and Barbara Dickson, Madonna and Paul Hardcastle (about the only innovative sound, with '19'). The following year – which saw *Infected* released – had 1960s star Cliff Richard in the top five best-sellers with 'Living Doll', alongside Diana Ross and Chris de Burgh. As Johnson returned to the UK in 1987, the highest-selling chart acts were Rick Astley, Starship and the Bee Gees. The final years of the 1980s would see the Stock, Aitken and Waterman production house – initially fronted by Australian pop star Kylie Minogue – achieve dominance. No wonder Johnson was in despair ... an emotion reinforced when his five-year relationship with Fiona Skinner collapsed.

Johnson's response was to throw himself into work. Talking on a 'making of' special on *Infected* on 24-hour music channel Music Box TV, Johnson talked about his next album: '[It] is probably going to be less political in some ways, more personal, because *Infected* ruined my personal life basically. It created a lot of problems because I've been so obsessed with my work, and I've neglected other areas of my life, and so the next album is probably going to be a love album.'

Later, Johnson outlined his approach to developing the material that became *Mind Bomb* to Dave Henderson in *Offbeat* magazine. 'Where I work, I'm surrounded by reference books, notepads and my instruments. Everything is there and I have a very simple way of working.' This workspace was in a new loft apartment he'd bought in Shoreditch, part of an effort to reconcile with Fiona Skinner.

In preparing for *Mind Bomb*, towards the end of 1987, Johnson had also decided it was time to put together a more traditional band for The The. He recruited several musicians he either knew, had worked with or had heard good things about. Both James Eller (bass guitar) and Dave Palmer (drums) were then working with Julian Cope on his third solo album (following The Teardrop Explodes), *Saint Julian* (1987, produced by Warne Livesey and featuring Tessa Niles on backing vocals). The fourth member was Johnson's old friend Johnny Marr, who had joined with Steven Morrissey in The Smiths rather than join The The back in 1982. With The Smiths having recently split, Marr – described by *The Guardian* as 'the 1980s' most inventive and distinctive guitarist' – was only too happy to take up the second chance offered by Johnson. This lineup would produce two studio albums – *Mind Bomb* (1989) and *Dusk* (1993) – and become Johnson's touring band. Eller would later return for 2024's *Ensoulment* (as did Livesey) and *Ensouled* world tour.

Johnson had been continuing his autodidactic self-education, reading widely. An atheist, he became fascinated by religion, not just Christianity but Islam and Buddhism. Although he set out to create a more personal album, the worlds of religion and politics could not help but intrude on his consciousness – he just had to watch the nightly news. His reading took in the Bible, the Quran, the Bhagavad Gita, and works by Walt Whitman, Carl Jung and Friedrich Nietzsche. Some of the songs on *Mind Bomb* would fuse religion and politics, seeing both as a means of control. There was still room for the more personal, relationship-based songs – such as 'Kingdom Of Rain', 'August & September' and 'Gravitate To Me' – a slight increase over the number featured on *Infected*.

Having resolved to clean up his act, Johnson went on a health kick, replacing drugs like cocaine and ecstasy with supposedly 'healthy' alternatives – like magic mushrooms – as a way of expanding his consciousness. Various diets and detox regimens were briefly adopted and quickly abandoned. By the time it came to working in the studio, vodka, ecstasy and cocaine had resumed their place in Johnson's drug intake, alongside the newer additions. '*Mind Bomb* was done on magic mushrooms', claimed Johnson. 'I had piles of books ... I was meditating ... doing all sorts of really deep, freakish things and getting into all this heavy Islamic stuff. Also Daoism, Buddhism, Hinduism, Judaism. I was trying ... to delve deeper into the world around me ... Everything [was] love and fear – all we see in this life is a manifestation of one of these opposing frequencies...'

While Johnson and his band were working on *Mind Bomb* in the studio in late summer and through the autumn of 1988, the underground music scene was changing. Although those connected with Stevo Pearce and Some Bizzare had been early adopters, it had taken a while for ecstasy to penetrate into the mainstream. Acid house music and warehouse 'rave' parties emerged as an alternative form of protest to the seemingly never-ending dominance of the Conservative government in 1980s Britain. Johnny Marr noted that 'Matt was resolutely ignoring the house scene, but I think that was him making sure he wasn't thrown off his course.'

It's possible Johnson saw acid house as an abdication of responsibility, a giving in to the desire to party as the country crumbled, something he'd become only too aware he'd earlier succumbed to. With *Mind Bomb*, he had much higher aspirations, as he told *Record Mirror* in 1989. 'Every day you're given choices, and the title *Mind Bomb* came about from what I would call splitting the moral atom, which is going so deep into yourself that you investigate the motive behind every desire and trace it right down deep within yourself. It's essentially the struggle between light and dark that goes on in everybody.' For the longest time, into early 1989, the working title for the new The The album had been *Psychonaut*, reflecting Johnson's own use of various substances to explore altered states of consciousness in an effort to discover the meaning of life. Instead, he lifted the much more explosive, dynamic *Mind Bomb* title from Timothy Leary's *Politics Of Ecstasy* (1968).

A bigger hit than *Infected*, *Mind Bomb* finally saw a The The album reach the top five (hitting number four, staying around for nine weeks). The reviews were hugely positive, with *Melody Maker* dubbing the album The The's equivalent of *Astral Weeks* (Van Morrison's second studio album), calling it 'a magnificent album, full of vital energy'. For *NME*, the band 'stretch[ed] their sound past the edge of madness it already inhabits', while *Sounds* dubbed *Mind Bomb* 'an enthralling album. The most complete The The record to date.' Again, America was also on board, with the *New York Times* commenting that 'the songs on *Mind Bomb* have a do-or-die urgency. Matt Johnson is a committed writer with something to say', and *Time* highlighting it as 'an album of furious energy and frustrated urgency'. Matt Johnson had successfully exploded his *Mind Bomb* on the music industry.

'Good Morning, Beautiful' 7:28
The opening track sets the tone, beginning like a fairy tale with a whispered vocal (delivered by producer Warne Livesey's young stepdaughter, Esmé Whybrow). Although disconnected from the rest of the song, the whispered voice (set against a background of Islamic calls to prayer and garbled communications chatter) focuses on all-encompassing surveillance. This was a topic that would inform later tracks like 'Global Eyes' on *Naked Self* and 'Kissing The Ring Of POTUS' on *Ensoulment*, among others. According to Johnny Marr's autobiography, both he and Johnson had indulged in some hallucinogenics, which led to an altered-state Johnson asking Marr to play the guitar 'like Jesus meets the Devil'. This theme – the battle between God and Satan, Christianity and Islam, the haves and the have-nots – picks up in 'Good Morning Beautiful' where *Infected* left off.

From that understated opening, the song plunges into a more muscular form, with Johnson delivering the piano line against the saxophones from Chris White and Phil Todd. It's a seven-and-a-half-minute epic that unfolds at a leisurely pace, with the vocals arriving over two minutes in. Johnson quickly establishes that the 'Devil' of legend is just the thoughts and desires that 'live in the human heart', not some supernatural entity. Almost spoken word in delivery, rather than singing, Johnson poses a series of questions, asking the listener to consider the sources of their information: 'Ask yourself/Whose voice is it/That whispers unto you?' Distortion on the 'Who is it?' line and those following sees Johnson adopting a demonic aspect in calling out 'the insanity of violence/And its brother, lust'.

As on *Infected*, the songs on *Mind Bomb*, epitomised by 'Good Morning Beautiful' (the title lifted from a slogan on a US egg carton), offer a dense, yet crisp and clear, production, allowing Marr and Eller's guitars not to be lost under all the other special effects, vocal and otherwise (even Mark Feltham's electronic harmonica is clearly heard in the mix). The thematic concern is on manipulation through religion, the media and politics: 'Whose words have been twisted/Beyond recognition/In order to build/Your planet Earth's religions?' There can be few songs that conclude by welcoming the end of the world with such delicious vocal harmony.

'Armageddon Days (Are Here Again)' 5:40

The first track recorded for *Mind Bomb* occupies the second slot. Having come to the conclusion, following close study of both the Bible and the Quran, that these different (and mutually antagonistic) religions were essentially singing from the same hymn book, he wrote 'Armageddon Days (Are Here Again)' to highlight that it was the distortions of the religious message by men that led to the world's wars. In that sense, its positioning following 'Good Morning Beautiful' makes perfect thematic sense – arranging the sequence of his songs was becoming ever more important to Johnson (especially following the unwanted addition of 'Perfect' to the US release of *Soul Mining*). In a sneaky bit of homage, drummer Dave Palmer aped the drum pattern of glam rock classic 'Ballroom Blitz' by Sweet, while Johnson picked up on the notion of introducing Jesus, Buddha and Mohamed as Sweet had introduced the band members (the sleeve credits listed Eller, Marr and Palmer as the voices of 'the prophets').

It's another highly political song, opulent and cinematic in its presentation, building on the work Johnson and Livesey had achieved with *Infected*. As relevant today as back in the 1980s, the chorus lines remain pertinent: 'Islam is rising/The Christians mobilising/The world is on its elbows and knees/It's forgotten the message/And worship's the creed'. An entire verse on the Falklands conflict ('It's war, she cried' can only be a reference to Thatcher) ends on the couplet 'You'll watch the ships sail out of the harbour/And the bodies come floating back'. Audio extracts from the fatal shooting of Robert Kennedy in 1968 ('get the gun/stay away from the gun') play behind the robust guitars and drums. The entire piece is given a sublime grandeur by the addition of the Ambrosian Singers choir and the Astari Strings, alongside

Gavin Wright's Arabian fiddle. It lifts the piece as it builds to a conclusion with Johnson almost shouting, 'Armageddon days are here again'. Livesey recalled the male voice choir singing the lines on Islam and Christianity: 'They were all middle-aged gentlemen who were used to singing on operatic and classical records.'

Operatic was certainly the feel that Johnson and Livesey were going for with 'Armageddon Days (Are Here Again)', and given all that was going on in the world then, it was the obvious choice as the first single. It wasn't to be, however, as the record company got cold feet about releasing such a potentially contentious song in the wake of the Salman Rushdie fatwa affair of 1989, where the Ayatollah of Iran issued an Islamic execution order on the author for his novel *The Satanic Verses*. Instead, 'Armageddon Days (Are Here Again)' became the third single, released on 7 October 1989, but it only spent two weeks in the UK Single Charts, reaching a disappointing number 70. The opening combo of 'Good Morning Beautiful' and 'Armageddon Days (Are Here Again)' made for an epic one-two punch to launch *Mind Bomb*.

'The Violence Of Truth' 5:40

The contentious themes and muscular, dynamic production continue right into 'The Violence Of Truth', which opens with more 'found media' audio connecting religion and material desire. Religion and its distortion are once again centre-stage, with 'God' seemingly the most repeated word in the first three songs. The central point of 'The Violence Of Truth' comes in the lines: 'Why is it that anything on this Earth/We do not understand/We are pushed down on our knees/To worship or to damn?' It's a hard-edged, swirling track that gets to the core of Johnson's 'good versus evil' battle lines. Truth and lies become confused ('God is evil/God is love'), while falling in line is to be avoided ('The dangers of obedience/The violence of truth'). Surveillance again rears its head ('Where is the force that watches over you?') and religion is seen as oppressive ('Those are the rules of religion/Those are the laws of the land/That's how the forces of darkness/Have suppressed the spirit of man').

Musically, Livesey pushes things further, giving a sharper feel to Marr's distorted, grinding 'wah-wah' guitar and allowing 'Wix' Wickens' Hammond organ to lead in conjunction with Mark Feltham's harmonica, followed by Palmer's muscular drums. There's more than a simple echo of the song 'Infected' here, as Johnson employs a very similar guitar riff, albeit sped up (driven by the urgency of the vocal delivery) and distorted.

Moving on from the perhaps more-of-its-time musical construction of *Infected*, the first three tracks on *Mind Bomb* deliver a sequence of timeless, indeed prophetic, songs that raised issues in 1989 that the world is still confronting a quarter of the way into the 21st century. There is little that is dated here, either in the music or the lyrics – both have stood the test of time.

Above: Matt Johnson – the creative driving force behind The The – in full flow at Glastonbury in 2000 (*Alamy*)

Left: The cover of Johnson's first ever album, *See Without Being Seen*, released initially on cassette in 1978 but reissued on CD in 2020. (*Cineola*)

Right: The cover for Johnson's first commercial album, *Burning Blue Soul* (1981), featuring the distinctive art of his brother Andrew 'Andy Dog' Johnson. (*Warner Bros./4AD*)

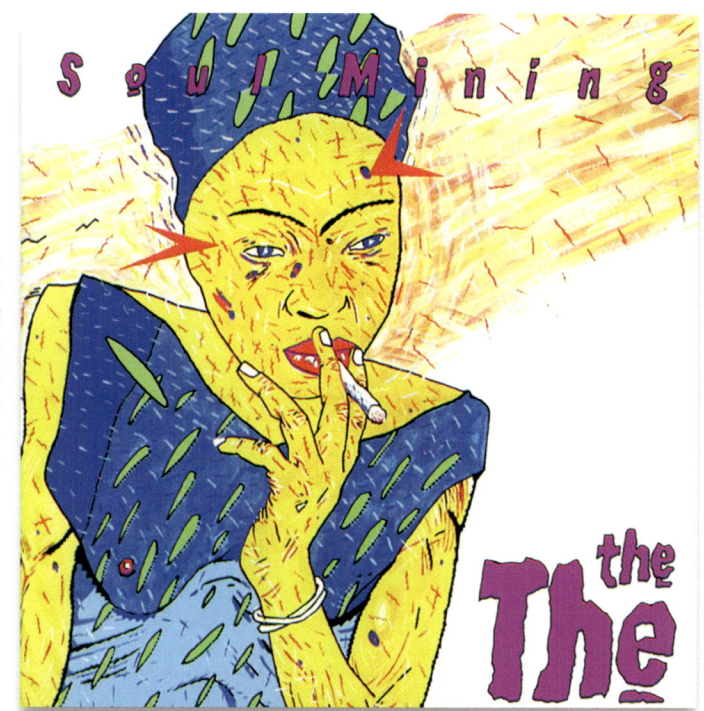

Right: Further 'Andy Dog' art for the successful *Soul Mining* (1983) album, modelled after a photo of one of Fela Kuti's wives. (*Some Bizzare/Epic*)

Left: One of the defining albums of the 1980s, *Infected* (1986) was a multi-media project including *Infected: The Movie*. (*Some Bizzare/Epic*)

Above: Early collaborators Marc Almond and Matt Johnson in 1982 – both connected with wayward manager Stevo Pearce. (*Janette Beckman/Getty Images*)

Right: On the cusp of success – Matt Johnson in 1983, just as *Soul Mining* was released. (*Gentle Look via Getty Images*)

Below: Matt Johnson in 1982, chronicling London bedsit life in the 1980s through songs like 'The Twilight Hour'. (*Joelle Depont*)

Left: A moment from the much-seen pop video for The The's best-known single 'This Is The Day' from the *Soul Mining* album.

Right: A face-painted Matt Johnson as an Andy Dog illustration come-to-life in the video for 'Angels Of Deception'.

Left: Johnson fearlessly engaged with the international politics of the 1980s in songs and videos like the anti-US 'Angels Of Deception'.

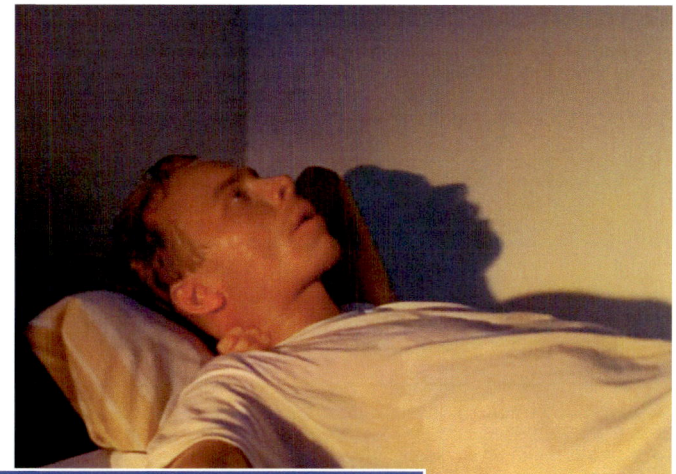

Right: During the making of the video for 'The Mercy Beat' in South America, Johnson recalled being 'so high' while filming ...

Left: 'Western guy' Matt Johnson heads towards a confrontation with the Devil in the epic video for 'The Mercy Beat'.

Right: Johnson was caught up in a crowd of communist rebels while filming the music video for 'The Mercy Beat' in Bolivia.

Left: The simple, distinctive cover for 1989's *Mind Bomb*, featuring a shaven-headed Johnson, which reached the top five in the UK Album Chart. (*Epic*)

Right: Andrew Johnson contributed art for the cover of The The's *Dusk*, an emotion-driven chronicle of life in London town from 1993. (*Sony*)

Right: Johnson does Hank Williams in his unlikely 1995 album of cover versions, *Hanky Panky*, which grew from plans for an EP. (*550 Music/Epic*)

Left: The minimalist but atmospheric cover for 2000's *Naked Self*, an album rejected by Sony as lacking in commercial value... (*Nothing/Universal*)

Above: The 1989 lineup for the *Mind Bomb* album and tour – drummer David Palmer, Johnny Marr, Matt Johnson and James Eller.

Below: The much-expanded *Dusk*-era live lineup of The The in 1993 – including Marr and Eller, alongside Johnson. (*Chris Buck*)

Right: A poster for the 2017 film *The Inertia Variations*, which charted Matt Johnson's creative block in the early 21st century. (*Johanna St Michaels*)

Below: Matt Johnson charted the changing nature of his London environment in the 2017 film *The Inertia Variations*. (*Johanna St Michaels*)

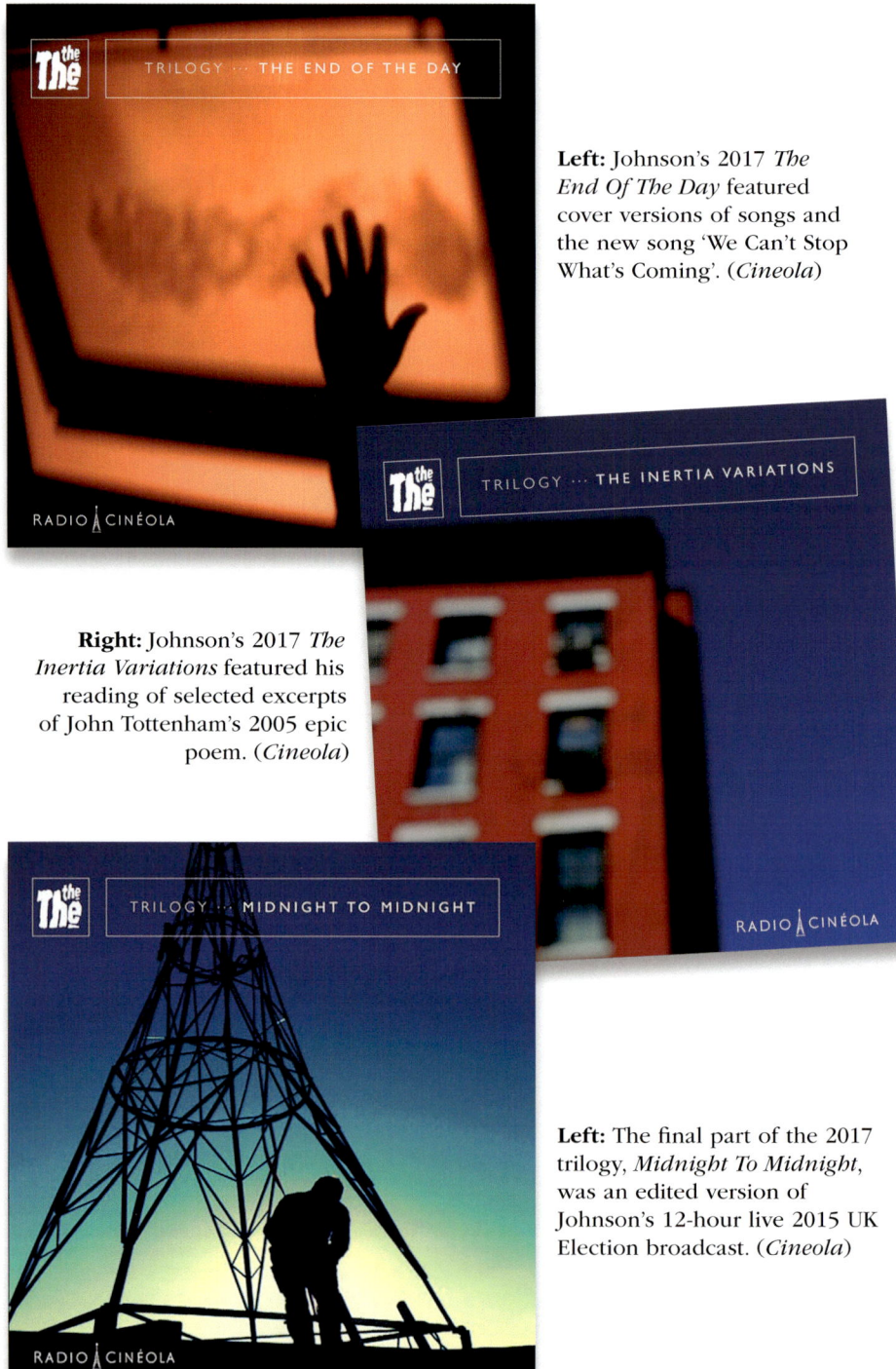

Left: Johnson's 2017 *The End Of The Day* featured cover versions of songs and the new song 'We Can't Stop What's Coming'. (*Cineola*)

Right: Johnson's 2017 *The Inertia Variations* featured his reading of selected excerpts of John Tottenham's 2005 epic poem. (*Cineola*)

Left: The final part of the 2017 trilogy, *Midnight To Midnight*, was an edited version of Johnson's 12-hour live 2015 UK Election broadcast. (*Cineola*)

Right: Matt Johnson's first movie soundtrack was for his brother Gerard's film *Tony* (2009), released on his own Cineola label. (*Cineola*)

Left: For *Hyena* (2014), Johnson employed familiar The The sounds (especially from *Dusk*) to capture a threatening version of London's underworld. (*Cineola*)

Right: For the soundtrack of Nichola Bruce's documentary *Moonbug* (2010), Johnson utilised tape loops, piano, synths, guitars and percussion for an other-worldly sound. (*Cineola*)

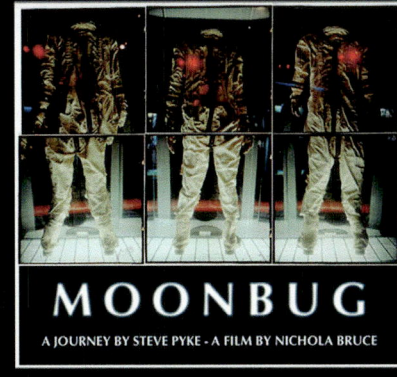

Above: Matt Johnson with long-term collaborator Johnny Marr playing at The National Bowl on 22 June 2025 in Milton Keynes. (*Jim Dyson/Getty Images*)

Below: Matt Johnson performing at London's Royal Albert Hall during The The's long-awaited return to live performance in 2018. (*Getty*)

Above: Matt Johnson, ensconced in his home studio where all the most recent The The releases have been created.

Below: Matt Johnson (centre) leads the 2018 The The lineup: Barrie Cadogan, DC Collard, Earl Harvin and James Eller. (*John Claridge*)

Left: The The's first album of original songs in almost 25 years, 2024's *Ensoulment*, featured unused art by the late Andrew 'Andy Dog' Johnson. (*Cineola/earMusic*)

Right: The The's 'I Want 2 B U', from the soundtrack of Gerard Johnson's 2019 film *Muscle*, featured further Andy Dog art. (*Cineola*)

'Kingdom Of Rain' 5:51

After all the politics and religion, Johnson offers some respite with the change-of-pace side one closer, 'Kingdom Of Rain'. We're back to the personal, following up *Infected*'s 'Slow Train To Dawn' with another relationship-focused duet with a rising female vocalist, Sinead O'Connor. Inspired by Johnson's own fame-and-success-driven infidelities and the collapse of his relationship with Fiona Skinner, 'Kingdom Of Rain' is an atmospheric narrative track (opening with weather sound effects) that gets inside the heads of its protagonists. Over the years, the pair grow apart but neither seems able to quit the other: 'You were the girl I wanted to cry with/You were the girl I wanted to die with/And you were the boy who turned into the man/Broke my heart and let go of my hand'. Acoustic guitars feature, while the percussion draws upon more unusual instruments like bongos and congas.

Johnson first encountered O'Connor when he saw her in a music video on a television with the sound turned down – it was her unusual shaven-headed look that caught his attention. 'I just had a feeling about her', he said. '[I] knew I needed her to duet with me ... It was a real bonus when I ... found out how good a singer she was.' O'Connor's vocal gives new life to Johnson's own, as he delivers a much more laid-back song, even if the lyrics are driven by anguish: 'Our bed is empty/The fire is out/And all the love we've got to give/Is all spurted out'. If nothing else, Johnson was always big on self-lacerating lyrics when it came to the subjects of love, sex, romance, desire and lust.

The element of time and its impact on long-running relationships is echoed by Eller's tricky bassline and Palmer's rimshots and condensed in the lyrics with the lines: 'You move further from my side, year by year/While still making love, dutifully sincere' alongside 'And I would lie awake and wonder/'Is it just me? Or is this the way that love is/Supposed to be?". The kingdom of rain that is their emotional lives comes to a climax with the return of the stormy weather soundtrack, featuring rain and thunder and even some displaced whale song.

Producer Warne Livesey hoped that 'Kingdom Of Rain' would be a single, with its strong vocal performance from both Johnson and O'Connor. However, it was O'Connor who blocked such a release as she didn't want anything to distract from her forthcoming album, which featured a potential single of its own in 'Nothing Compares 2 U'. That track would become the late O'Connor's signature song, spending four weeks at number one on the chart in 1990. 'Kingdom Of Rain' did receive a 7" and a 12" release as a promo-only single in the US, Australia and the Netherlands.

'The Beat(en) Generation' 3:04

Perhaps side two opener 'The Beat(en) Generation' would have been better served as the closer to side one, with 'Kingdom Of Rain' moved to side two, thus neatly splitting the political/religious side one from the more relationship-driven side two. Clearly, Johnson didn't want such a bald split between the two sides of *Mind Bomb* as he refused to implement what looks like a (perhaps too) obvious arrangement of the material.

It was a rough demo of 'The Beat(en) Generation' that Johnson played to Johnny Marr on the night that he persuaded The Smiths' guitarist to join The The. When it came to recording, this was one of the first tracks laid down in the initial sessions for *Mind Bomb*. Marr was ready to play the guitar part 'off the top of his head' (according to producer Warne Livesey – 'That was it, job done!'). As with the recording of 'Good Morning Beautiful', drugs were again in evidence during the sessions, except this time it was ecstasy, which had gained hugely in mainstream acceptance long after the early access enjoyed by Stevo Pearce and the Some Bizzare gang.

Although political in content, the lyrics of 'The Beat(en) Generation' steered away from the globe-spanning concerns (and aggressive production) of the first three tracks. This was a return to the territory so bitingly explored on 'Heartland' (and before that on 'I've Been Waiting For Tomorrow (All Of My Life)' and 'The Sinking Feeling'). The lyrics have bite ('We're being sedated by the gasoline fumes/And hypnotised by the satellites/Into believing what is good and what is right'), but the musicality is a lot lighter, even sprightly, compared to the aggressive opening tracks. The song is about the corruption of youthful ambition by the older political establishment, who see the youth as nothing but fodder (whether for foreign wars or the factories). That's all clear when Johnson sings: 'And our youth, oh youth, are being seduced/By the greedy hands of politics and half truths'. Johnson was an early adopter in tackling disinformation, whether from newspapers, television or directly from politicians, a very 21st-century concern he would explore in even greater depth on *Naked Self* and *Ensoulment*.

Like many of his earlier songs, Johnson wraps up his hard-edged sentiments in the lightest of pop tunes, perfectly suitable to Marr's jangling guitar and harmonica playing. 'Wix' Wickens performs the piano line and adds to the background with some fine accordion work. Johnson, Livesey and Marr are joined on the backing vocals by Geoff Foster, while Livesey also plays the acoustic guitar.

Released as the first single from *Mind Bomb*, 'The Beat(en) Generation' suggested a change of direction for The The from the majority of the material on *Infected*, a smoother, gentler, more 'pop' approach which was not followed through on the album itself. In that way, 'The Beat(en) Generation' was an odd choice for a single (released on 1 April 1989), not being representative of the album. However, its similarity – musically and lyrically – to 'Heartland' was probably the deciding factor, and the single saw the band breach the top 20 for the first time, hitting number 18 (significantly higher than 'Heartland's number 29) and remaining in the UK Singles Chart for a decent five weeks.

'August & September' 5:45

The final trio of tracks explore personal relationships, love and lust, opening with the lyrical 'August & September'. This was another song that saw Johnson draw directly upon his now on-and-off relationship with Fiona Skinner. It chronicles the growing distance between a man and a woman in an intimate relationship. It charts the anguish of love, the torture of separation and the possibilities of reconciliation in a romantic manner, yet Johnson can't resist turning on himself with the chilling conclusion to the song.

Opening at a slower pace with the piano of 'Wix' Wickens once more to the fore, the song extends its instrumentation beyond the usual guitar-and-drums combo by enlisting significant wind instrumentation (clarinet, bass clarinet, and oboe) and the return of a string section, arranged and conducted by Andrew Poppy. It once more pulls off that Johnson trick of disguising critical lyrics within appealing music. Dave Palmer uses brushes on the drums, adding to the initial lightness before the song gives way to a horrifying climax.

The song's title comes from the two months Johnson and Skinner spent apart while considering their future. Johnson – as so often before, whether from personal experience (as here) or in the abstract – poured out his heart and explored his own suffering through lyrics like 'Your life with me was ending/Your new life had begun', bolstered by the self-critical 'And I was praying for the strength/To stop loving you'. That these emotions play out on the surface (Johnson's vocal is at the top of the mix) of such stirring music is what makes 'August & September' one of The The's best tracks. The reasonableness of the song's opening sections soon turns to self-flagellation and self-justification, putting male desires and needs above all else. Each instrumental section between the developing narrative story emphasises the light music before plunging back into an ever darker narrative.

Talking to Neil Fraser, Dave Palmer recalled how such a simple-sounding ballad-style song took a while to come together. 'You couldn't really punch in on it … the brushes are constantly moving', said Palmer. 'We had to really nail it, and Matt was searching for something … he wanted it delicate, kind of humble, almost falling apart. It took us a while.' The 'falling apart' comes at the climax, as things take a darker turn (prefaced by screams deep in the mix), both lyrically and musically (and in the treatment of Johnson's wrought vocals). From his recognition of both parties' responsibility ('Was our love too strong to die?/Or were we just too weak to kill it?') to justifying his own obsessional needs ('What kind of man was I?/Who would sacrifice your happiness to satisfy his pride?' and 'Who could delay your destiny to appease his/Screaming little mind?'), Johnson's angry male 'screaming mind' is given full throttle in the distortion of the shouted 'You're mine!' line that wraps up the track in a chilling manner.

'Gravitate To Me' 8:09 (Matt Johnson, Johnny Marr)

A co-write with Johnny Marr, 'Gravitate To Me' was one of the handful of The The tracks that wasn't a solo Johnson creation. Anything following the dramatic finale of 'August & September' was perhaps doomed to seem somehow lesser, but Johnson made a smart choice in positioning the contemplative (though no less lustful) 'Gravitate To Me' here. The old melodica is dug out, while Ashley Slater weighs in with the trombone. Eller and Marr get to play around almost wistfully and whimsically with their guitar work, as if the pressure was off. This song suggests a band relaxing into the instrumentation, in a less precise, less specific way than Johnson usually pursued. The co-writing credit on the music for Marr suggests some degree of improvisation or jamming may have been involved in the development process.

The self-recriminations of both 'Kingdom Of Rain' and 'August & September' are forgotten here, as Johnson once more plays the part of a lustful fella who is out to get what he thinks he deserves. The base motivation of sex is dressed up in some high-faluting notion of reincarnation ('For we are kindred spirits/Born to become Earthly lovers' and the chorus lines of 'I know you/ From a previous incarnation'). It was a subject that Johnson often toyed with and may have come from some form of personal belief that was to come to fuller fruition on several tracks on 2024's *Ensoulment*.

Released as the second single from *Mind Bomb* (on 22 July 1989, when 'Kingdom Of Rain' may have been more suitable), 'Gravitate To Me' crashed and burned, reaching number 63 in the UK Singles Chart and sticking around for four weeks, quite a contrast to 'The Beat(en) Generation's earlier penetration of the top 20. The single edit at 4:32 (backed by 'The Violence Of Truth' on the B-side) is a briefer, sharper take on the material in comparison to the over eight-minute indulgence of the album cut.

'Beyond Love' 4:22
The final track continues the unexpected mellow mood of 'Gravitate To Me'. With 'Beyond Love', Johnson returns once again to sex and love. Wrapping up the album in some style, 'Beyond Love' is an appeal for a higher meaning, something beyond the physical. There's the selfish justification of desire ('There are some things in this life/That you just can't fight/It's as if the spirits above/Have cast a little spell upon us') and the removal of the limits of religion as a restraint ('So let us take off our crosses/And lay them in a tin/ And let our weakness become virtue/Instead of a sin'). The crude physical movements of mere copulation ('In and out like the tide') are simply a gateway to a higher state of being ('Take me beyond love/Up to something above/Take me to a happiness/Beyond human reach'). It's familiar Johnson stuff, couched in his usual carefully crafted lyrics. There is, however, an echo of the seediness of 'Out Of The Blue (Into The Fire)' in the lines 'The drops of semen/And the clots of blood/Which may, one day/Become like us' that undermines the romance. All this is – naturally – in the service of selfish desires, the need to know oneself through physical interaction with another: 'I'll take you to the angels/If you'll take me to myself.' A more sedate song

than most on *Mind Bomb*, more like a ballad, 'Beyond Love' is introduced by John Eacott's wistful flugelhorn and closes on an upbeat, almost evangelical note as it fades away.

At just over four minutes, 'Beyond Love' is a blissed-out conclusion that doesn't outstay its welcome. Johnson had definite aims for 'Beyond Love' that he was never quite sure he pulled off. 'It was an attempt at expressing a metaphysical idea more than it was a love song. Lyrically, it is one of the most important songs on the album. I was trying to express metaphysical ideas about the world of illusion and duality we're trapped in. The line 'Let us take off our crosses...' is an invitation to leave religious dogma behind and embrace our true instincts and nature ... This song is simply a yearning to reach beyond love and the illusory world of duality and suffering that we're trapped inside and 'Up to something above'.' That could stand as a summing up of the themes and approaches that suffuse *Mind Bomb*, but it was also a dip of the toe into the metaphysical waters that Johnson would come to explore in much more depth in *Ensoulment*.

Related Tracks
'Jealous Of Youth' 4:18 (single), 6:42 (extended)
Released between *Mind Bomb* and *Dusk*, the *Shades Of Blue* EP served several purposes. It promoted the then-underway tour, *The The Versus The World*, which saw a previously reluctant Johnson embark on an epic number of live dates with his bandmates. The first track on the four-track EP, 'Jealous Of Youth' (produced by Roli Mosimann), was released as a 7" single for the US market in February 1990 (backed by the *Mind Bomb* closer 'Beyond Love' and a 12" extended 'Jealous Of Youth'). It had been considered for a slot on *Mind Bomb*, but Johnson had preferred to include 'Gravitate To Me' instead.

Opening with a spoken word section, the song emerges as a guitar-driven exploration of nostalgia. As so often, Johnson uses the seasons to denote the passing of time: 'But now the autumn leaves are turning to the colour of rust/I'm getting jealous for youth's first yearnings for lust'. The first verse recounts a night of youthful love (or lust) ('I was once her man/At the midnight hour'), but later verses move on to criticise the demonisation of the 'other', those from cultures or religions not our own: 'Yet it's funny how as we grow old/We curse and point our finger at those/Those! Those! Those!/Who made us scared and made us old'. As ever, Johnson was prescient, exploring issues that have only become ever more important with the rise of populist political figures like Nigel Farage in the UK and Donald Trump in the US. There's also the usual note of self-criticism about the singer's own inertia and inability to achieve anything ('I want to live/I want to live/But I ain't a big enough man to do anything other than think'), a feeling that would ultimately come to swamp Johnson's own creativity for the first decade or so of the 21st century.

Released in the UK as the *Shades Of Blue* EP (with the three following tracks, below), it spent two weeks in the UK Singles Chart, reaching a high of number 54.

'Another Boy Drowning (Live)' 6:11
A live recording of the final track from Johnson's first official album, *Burning Blue Soul*.

'Solitude' 2:42 (Duke Ellington, Eddie DeLange, Irving Mills)
A cover version of the 1934 Duke Ellington tune, '(In My) Solitude' was a piano-based track whose title and theme were a natural for Johnson and makes a fitting partner for 'Jealous Of Youth'. It had previously been recorded over the decades in various versions as an Ellington instrumental or an Ellington piano solo, with the vocal performed by Louis Armstrong (plus horns), Billie Holiday or Ella Fitzgerald. The jazz standard – with music by Ellington and lyrics by Eddie DeLange and Irving Mills – obviously appealed to Johnson, given the wistful lyrical content and tinkling musicality. Ellington claimed to have composed it in just 20 minutes, creating a sombre piece that nonetheless remains optimistic and upbeat. A version of the song reached number two in the US Charts in 1935.

Over the decades, '(In My) Solitude' had been covered by Josephine Baker, Tony Bennett, Oscar Peterson and sundry others, so Johnson was joining a starry procession. He was no doubt struck by the way the lyrics echoed many of his own preoccupations, from *Burning Blue Soul* onwards. After all, is there a more The The suitable lyric than the song's opening lines, 'In my solitude/You haunt me/With dreadful ease/Of days gone by'? Or even the bed-sit suitable 'I sit in my chair/And filled with despair/There's no one could be so sad'? Johnson tampered with (or 'revised') the lyrics a bit, replacing 'With dreadful ease' with a more pleasing 'With reveries' that flows better to the modern ear (and dropped '(In My)' from the title). Johnson adopts a whispery vocal, which becomes stronger and more emphatic as the song proceeds. This track and the following cover version of Fred Neil's 'The Dolphins' may have planted the seeds in Johnson's mind for *Hanky Panky*, his unexpected 1995 album of Hank Williams cover versions.

'Dolphins' 4:10 (Fred Neil)
Similarly, 'Dolphins' is a cover of a folk rock song (originally 'The Dolphins') from 1967 written by American singer-songwriter Fred Neil and featured on his self-titled second solo album. Although the original lyrics featured the line 'I've been searching for the dolphins in the sea', it was intended as a more abstract song, rather than one about sea life. However, Neil did go on to establish the Dolphin Research Project with Ric O'Barry in 1970, an organisation dedicated to the protection of dolphins. The song was frequently performed by Tim Buckley, though he didn't lay down a recorded

version until 1973, just two years before his untimely drug overdose death at the age of 28.

'The Dolphins' became a folk rock standard with several notable cover versions including those by Linda Ronstadt, Harry Belafonte, Billy Bragg and Eddi Reeder. Again, the lyrics appealed to Johnson. There's the timeless politics ('This old world may never change/The way it's been/And all the ways of war/Can't change it back again'), the near forgotten romance ('I've been searching/For the dolphins in the sea/And sometimes I wonder/Do you ever think of me?') and the personal reminiscence ('You know sometimes I think about/Saturday's child/And all about the time/When we were running wild'). That latter sentiment would be central to the spoken word track 'Down By The Frozen River' on *Ensoulment*, and in his version of 'Dolphins' (no 'The', ironically), Johnson moved those last two elements to the top of the song, as they were more personally meaningful to him. He also adapts 'This old world may never change' to the more definitive 'This old world will never change'. The track concludes with a neat Marr guitar solo.

Dusk (1993)

Personnel:
Matt Johnson: lead vocals, electric guitar, acoustic guitar, keyboards
Johnny Marr: electric guitar, acoustic guitar, harmonica, backing vocals
James Eller: bass guitar
David Palmer, Vinnie Colaiuta, Bruce Smith: drums
D. C. Collard: keyboards
Danny Thompson: upright bass on 'This Is The Night'
John Thirkell: trumpet on 'Helpline Operator'
David Lawrence: flugelhorn on 'Lung Shadows'
Ashley Slater: trombone on 'Lung Shadows'
Chris Batchelor: trumpet on 'Lung Shadows'
Guy Barker: trumpet on 'Bluer Than Midnight'
Paul Webb, Zeke Manyika: chorus on 'Lonely Planet'
Recorded at The Garden, London, between summer and autumn 1992
Producers: Matt Johnson, Bruce Lampcov
Label: Sony
Release date: 25 January 1993 (UK)
Charts: UK: 2, US: 138, Aus: 20, Austria: 28, Netherlands: 37, Germany: 23, New Zealand: 6, Norway: 10, Sweden: 15, Switzerland: 20
Running time: 41:02
All tracks written by Matt Johnson

In order to promote *Mind Bomb*, Matt Johnson finally committed to taking The The on tour. For the first time since *Burning Blue Soul*, Johnson's face appeared on the *Mind Bomb* sleeve. CBS/Sony got behind the promotional effort in a bigger way now that The The resembled a recognisable group. One attraction the label wanted to capitalise on was The Smiths' Johnny Marr being a crucial part of the lineup. Much of the promotional material around the *Mind Bomb* era consisted of moody black-and-white shots of the foursome that now made up the core of The The.

Another change had been Johnson's parting of the ways with Stevo Pearce and Some Bizzare. Stevo's increasingly erratic behaviour was proving to be more of a liability than an asset to Johnson's career. 'When I eventually fired him,' said Johnson, 'I sat down with him face-to-face and told him as directly, but sensitively, as I could. Consequently, he wasn't involved in any way, shape or form in the writing, recording or promotion of *Mind Bomb*.' This pushed Johnson to take his career more seriously, to re-evaluate promotion and led to taking the band on tour.

The process of creating *Mind Bomb* had solidified the individual members of The The – Johnson, Marr, James Eller and David Palmer – into a cohesive unit. They worked well together in the studio, so it seemed only sensible – after nearly a decade of avoiding live performing – for The The to hit the road. News of the *The The Versus The World* tour was announced prior to the album's release. The only element missing from the lineup was a reliable keyboard player. Paul 'Wix' Wickens, who'd played on *Mind Bomb*, was invited to join the tour, but was already committed to working with The Beatles' Paul McCartney. Taking his place was D. C. 'Dave' Collard, who'd played with The Subway Sect and JoBoxers. His audition consisted of replicating the Jools Holland piano solo from 'Uncertain Smile'. He'd become an important addition to The The.

The The Versus The World would run for a full 12 months, taking in almost 100 shows spread across 21 countries – this from a man who'd rarely played live and, in many of his autobiographical songs, claimed to be 'disorganised'. The rest of his band had more touring experience, but that only made Johnson more determined. Other members, like Marr, appreciated Johnson's newfound commitment to serious organisation, and the tour proved to be a great showcase for a very slick band (who'd rehearsed extensively) playing a variety of tracks from *Soul Mining*, *Infected* and *Mind Bomb*. Odd 'homeless' tracks like 'Flesh And Bones' and 'Jealous Of Youth' found a place in the set list, while 'Another Boy Drowning' would be the only song from *Burning Blue Soul* (re-released under The The branding in 1993, at the same time as *Dusk*).

While on a break, Johnson received the shock news that his youngest brother Eugene had died suddenly of a ruptured brain aneurysm. It was a devastating moment for the Johnson family. There was no choice but to delay the next leg of the tour. This personal loss would feed into the writing of The The's next album, 1993's *Dusk*, with Johnson using songwriting as a way of not only coping with his grief (and that of his wider family) but also turning it to something creative.

The finale of the world tour came with a three-night sold-out residence at London's Royal Albert Hall. Tim Pope recorded these concerts, released almost a year later on VHS as *The The Versus The World*, a film that captured this incarnation of the band at their height. Despite the tragedy that had disrupted the tour, Johnson knew he was wrapping up the *Mind Bomb* era on a high. 'I was really exhausted', recalled Johnson. 'I just sat back with a nice contented feeling of a job well done.' The concert video, like *Infected: The Movie*, remains trapped in legal limbo with no release on DVD.

An even harder to see The The film is the Tim Pope-directed *From Dusk 'Til Dawn*. Shot in the wake of *Dusk*, the film was a mix of gonzo-style documentary and an extended music video. Pope, Johnson and Marr wandered New York asking various deep questions and met up with underground celebrities, such as Annie Sprinkle (in pre-arranged encounters). Shot on 16mm film in grainy black-and-white, the result was an oblique way of promoting either the band or the album, but was in line with *Infected: The Movie* and *The The Versus The World* in the way Johnson used film. This would ultimately lead to him exploring film music and working closely with his film director younger brother, Gerard. As with the previous two films,

From Dusk 'Til Dawn saw a limited VHS release, only to vanish thereafter. For *Dusk*, Pope also helmed a trio of videos: 'Dogs Of Lust', 'Slow Emotion Replay' and 'Love Is Stronger Than Death', the latter shot in New Orleans. He wouldn't shoot another The The video until 'Pillar Box Red' in 2002.

During the tour, the band had committed to recording another album, this time with D. C. Collard as a full member. Johnson had used John Foxx's London studio, The Garden, to record the *Shades Of Blue* EP, which included the two melancholy covers. Johnson had taken such a liking to The Garden that he decided to buy it, while also starting on the writing of the next album. D. C. Collard worked closely on the demos for *Dusk*, declaring the finished record to be 'pretty true to those demos'. The demos were so carefully constructed that when it came time to record in the summer of 1992, everything went off smoothly. Meticulous months of preparation meant that the recording only took two weeks. Johnson insisted on a particular atmosphere, matching the new songs. 'I wanted an intense, sleazy vibe', he admitted. 'I ensured the studio was extremely dark and hot with incense burning and oil wheels slowly turning. We were all relaxed in each other's company. I wanted the album to feel more stripped down [than the bombastic *Mind Bomb*].'

Hired as producer was Bruce Lampcov, who'd remixed *Mind Bomb*'s 'Gravitate To Me' for the 12" and had recorded the *The The Versus The World* shows in Detroit. Johnson saw Lampcov as ideal to ensure the new record captured this band lineup's 'live' feel. In particular, 'Dogs Of Lust' was a raucous song that benefited from being recorded largely 'as live'. 'It was one of those records,' recalled Lampcov, 'where everything seemed to come together exactly as it should.'

Dusk wasn't trouble-free. Drummer Dave Palmer was let go halfway through due to his inability to turn up on time and on the right day, thanks to extended clubbing and substance abuse. Vinnie Colaiuta – touring with Sting – was recruited to hit the skins on 'Dogs Of Lust' after Palmer's ouster. Thereafter, Colaiuta split sticks duty with The Pop Group's Bruce Smith. Palmer appeared on four of the ten tracks, with Colaiuta and Smith on two others. The remainder, including opener 'True Happiness This Way Lies', lacked drums altogether. Palmer's departure was an early indication of the forthcoming disintegration of the band's most successful lineup.

With *Dusk*, Johnson reached a creative peak. He had the right collaborators at the right time to produce his finest work. Sales were brisk, even if short-lived, propelling *Dusk* into the UK Album Chart at number two – making it The The's second top five album, bettering *Mind Bomb*'s number four placement. The record's life in the charts was brief, vanishing completely after just four weeks. Nothing subsequently would match it, although 2024's *Ensoulment* would again crack the top 20. Only one of the singles – 'Dogs Of Lust' – reached the top 30.

Critically, the album also did well. *NME* scored *Dusk* 8/10, dubbing it a 'tingling, volatile, uninhibited near masterpiece … a rich and hugely rewarding experience.' *Q* concurred: 'Johnson is something of a musical miracle worker. A very enjoyable record indeed.' *Melody Maker* singled out specific tracks: 'Songs like 'Slow Emotion Replay', 'Dogs Of Lust' and particularly 'Helpline Operator' are among the finest [from] the wordsmiths of his generation. If anything, [Johnson's] creative powers are very much in the ascendant.' Style mag *i-D* dubbed Johnson 'a post-Thatcher John Lennon', while *Select* labelled *Dusk* 'a masterful panorama of millennial angst.' *Smash Hits* even warmed to The The: 'Johnson has done it again. Chalk up another hit for the boy.' For *Vox*, Johnson's songs 'highlight his fascination with lust, failure, obsession and faulty communication in the urban world's twilight zone. Infectious throughout.'

Even the regular press approved, with *The Guardian* noting that 'Johnson's extraordinary voice scrapes the gravel of the soul one minute while rising confidently and boldly the next to fully realise the melodic possibilities. His best album in years.' Said the *Daily Telegraph*: '*Dusk*'s strength and force comes from Johnson's apparent sincerity', while *The Sunday Times* noted the new work was 'more stylish than anything since 1983 masterpiece *Soul Mining*.'

Dusk struck a chord in America, with *Rolling Stone* declaring that Johnson 'displays his maturity as a songwriter. These are songs written in the language of raw need', while *Billboard* felt that 'The The hit a new creative peak with their most stripped down and most assured album to date.' The *Detroit Free Press* simply called *Dusk* 'The The's strongest and most consistent record to date ... further proof that pain can make great art.' *Buzz* offered a neat summation of Johnson's atmospheric work: 'Overall, *Dusk* is just what the name implies, the soothing chill of approaching evening upon the body after a long hot day.' The The member Johnny Marr agreed, in a 2013 interview with *Uncut* magazine: '*Dusk* is my favourite of the two The The records [I worked on] ... It's one of the few records I've made that I can detach myself from and just enjoy [it].'

During 1993, Johnson's band began to disintegrate. Palmer had been fired and Marr had moved on to collaborate with Bernard Sumner on Electronic. Several members had changed in their personal lives, with young families. The problem was that Johnson was committed (albeit reluctantly) to touring *Dusk*. With Collard the only remaining member alongside Johnson, Palmer was invited to rejoin for the tour (although he quit halfway through; he was replaced by Andy Kubiszewski). The trio took an apartment in New York and booked rehearsal rooms to audition replacement guitarists – the main audition piece was 'Dogs Of Lust'. Johnson had two possibilities in mind – Eric Schermerhorn or Dave Navarro. Unfortunately, both were otherwise occupied. Johnson finally settled on Keith Joyner, who, aged 24, became the youngest member of The The, a position usually held by Johnson.

Also recruited for the touring band were bassist Jared Nickerson and harmonica player Jim Fitting (who would work on *Hanky Panky*, with

Schermerhorn). *The Lonely Planet* tour was another epic, taking in around 90 dates worldwide; part of the tour saw The The playing support to Depeche Mode and New Order. A recording of a warm-up gig at Sony Studios in New York for MTV was released as a promo titled *Live In New York (Yeah, It's A Bootleg)*.

The Lonely Planet tour also finally saw the end of Johnson's on-and-off relationship with Fiona Skinner. The final break came when Skinner visited Johnson in San Francisco – according to Skinner's recollection, he seemed more interested in the band than in her, having not seen her for a month. The pair decided to separate. Johnson was already considering relocating to America – a country he loved for itself, if not for its foreign policy. There was one more mini-tour at the end of 1993, the *Jingle Hell* tour, made up of eight dates. For one, in Glasgow at the notorious Barrowlands, The The was joined on stage by the long-absent Marr. The tour wrapped up in late December, and Johnson spent an uncomfortable Christmas with Skinner. His move to New York and the start of a new era were just around the corner...

'True Happiness This Way Lies' 3:10

Dusk opens in stylish fashion with the heartfelt 'True Happiness This Way Lies', a song title that plays on the double meaning of the word 'Lies'. The treatment combines the needle-drop crackles-and-hiss of vinyl with the appreciative laughter of a club audience (both effects from a sound library). Johnson approaches the opening section as a spoken word piece, playing the part of a club MC talking directly to a live audience. It was a form he'd return to on 2024's *Ensoulment* on 'Down By The Frozen River' – a heavily autobiographical, entirely spoken word piece. Critic Pete Paphides – in a 2023 Medium post – summed up Johnson's lyrical approach after seeing him play live at the Royal Albert Hall in 2018: 'As the show reaches the apex of its arc, something else becomes apparent. You realise that Matt is, in effect, telling you the story of his life.' A strong strain of emotional autobiography runs through virtually all his work (especially evident in the relationship songs, rather than in the more bombastic political tracks).

In 'True Happiness This Way Lies', he's playing a character, but there is a deep well of personal experience that he's drawing upon when he comments on man's fickle nature. Having pursued the object of his (sexual/romantic) desire, the singer then admits: 'But when you put your arms around me/I'll be looking over your shoulder/For something new'. The attraction of the novel, the fresh, overrides what's already there. The opening section sets out the stall clearly – getting what you want ('the heart's desires') is no guarantee of contentment. Johnson was the only performer, a simple acoustic guitar his instrument. The song reaches an emotional climax that plays on the title: 'The only true freedom/Is freedom from the heart's desires/And the only true happiness ... this way lies'. Interviewed by Ken Micaleff, Johnson explored the track's soul-searching background: 'I've experimented with drugs, sex, alternative forms of health and medicine. They've all changed and added to me, but I still haven't found what I'm searching for ... Nothing seems to satisfy.' This opening track, and much of the rest of *Dusk*, came from a great deal of time in self-reflection following the death of Johnson's younger brother, Eugene. It was an event that would weave its way through all the songs on the album. 'True Happiness This Way Lies' is a short, punchy curtain raiser that displays new depths to Johnson's songwriting.

'Love Is Stronger Than Death' 4:38
Trying to derive meaning from Eugene's death, Johnson found solace in songs. He found writing new lyrics and music provided both an escape from himself and his grief, but also a way of processing it through his own creativity. This focus pushed *Dusk* in a very different, much more personal direction from *Mind Bomb*. A simple idea – it is love that defines life, and it is love that continues beyond death – drives the lyrics here. The first two lines – 'Me and my friend were walking/In the cold light of mourning' – are drawn directly from a real-life walk around Shoreditch Johnson took with Johnny Marr in the wake of Eugene's death. The audio pun of 'mourning' for 'morning' is a typical clever play on words from Johnson. The song explores all those missed opportunities that come to mind when someone dies: 'All the thoughts unuttered/All the feelings unexpressed'. It's not downbeat and works to a sublime positivity. Using the seasons – death of nature in winter, followed by new flowering in spring – Johnson suggests that the human spirit will overcome grief ('But awoken by grief, our spirits speak').

Johnson, singing and playing acoustic guitar, was joined on the track by Collard on the Hammond organ, Eller on bass guitar and Palmer on drums. Playing the harmonica that features so prominently was the 'friend' referenced in the song, Johnny Marr. 'There was no getting around the atmosphere put into that song', Marr recalled, noting that the whole thing was played through live two or three times and that was it. Gone was the complex post-production work that featured throughout *Mind Bomb*, replaced by emotional, live immediacy. 'I don't think we could have done more ... takes', said Marr. 'It was too intense ... We didn't discuss it, but we all knew what the song was [about].'

The third single released from *Dusk*, 'Love Is Stronger Than Death' reached a high of number 39 in the UK Singles Chart, right in the middle of its three-week presence between June and July 1993. *Melody Maker* – previously seemingly reluctant to praise Johnson – finally fell for his musical charms. '[Johnson]'s songs still speak for themselves', wrote Andrew Smith. 'He pens a melody, then lovingly imbues it with light and shade, like few others. 'Love Is Stronger Than Death' is excellent...'

The black and white music video was lifted from *From Dusk 'Til Dawn*, featuring filming in New Orleans, with the atmosphere adding something new to the song's lyrics. Scenes depict various family units, interspersed with a variety of medical situations (some of them perhaps suggesting the AIDS epidemic). The track was used over the end credits of the 1997 Gregg Araki film *Nowhere*, which depicts a day in the life of Los Angeles high school students as each undergoes strange experiences, from alien abduction to bad acid trips and sexual entanglements.

'Dogs Of Lust' 3:09
After the contemplative and deeply emotional opening tracks, *Dusk* takes a turn towards the rowdy and raucous with 'Dogs Of Lust', a song that plays like an off-cut from *Infected*, a sequel of sorts to 'Out Of The Blue (Into The Fire)'. Released as a single several months before the album, 'Dogs Of Lust' charted at number 25 upon release on 16 January 1993, holding that position in the second week before sliding down the chart over the next two weeks (number 33, number 57) before dropping out.

In *Details* magazine, Johnson revealed something evident to the many fans of The The who'd paid attention to his lyrics: 'I'm sometimes held ransom by my biological urges.' 'Dogs Of Lust' puts aside the spiritual for the physical, the need for lust to sometimes take the place of love. From the dirty, scuzzy guitars – provided by Johnson and Marr – to the sleazy lyrics ('When you're lustful/When you're lonely/And the heat is risin' slowly'), 'Dogs Of Lust' is a throwback to several earlier, earthier The The tracks echoing not only 'Out Of The Blue (Into The Fire)' but also 'Slow Train To Dawn' (*Infected*), 'August & September' and 'Beyond Love' (*Mind Bomb*). The insistent harmonica line – from Marr – was modelled by Johnson after an ambulance siren that provided unwitting inspiration as it sped past his Shoreditch flat. It's lyrically simple yet direct, confronting the sometimes difficult-to-control desire for instant gratification (usually through sex, but the 'need' can be applied to almost anything). Even the singer's attempt to control such desires is defeated by elements beyond his control – 'I keep reachin' up/But they drag me back down' – as if to suggest his 'better angels' are always defeated by base desires somehow separate ('they') from himself.

The video – by the ever-reliable Tim Pope – had to visually conjure up this 'heat', something taken literally when a trio of aircraft hangar heaters were used to overheat the band members, resulting in visible perspiration. Adding to the necessary feelings of loss of control, Johnson supplied his band with what he euphemistically dubbed 'tablets of 'medicine'' and doses of tequila. The result was one of Johnson's favourite music videos, a basic band performance with overlays and insert shots of a writhing woman to liven things up.

'Dogs Of Lust' did not go down well with the music press, with *Melody Maker* bizarrely dubbing it as 'inherently laughable as any other The The track', continuing oddly with 'it's way too clean and calculated.' *NME* took a more benevolent view, calling it 'a tingling, volatile, uninhibited near masterpiece.'

By the 1990s, The The tracks were becoming a staple of film and television soundtracks, especially following the creation of 'Darkness Falls' for the 1995 *Judge Dredd* movie. 'Dogs Of Lust' was a popular choice, with its noisy elements and raw lyrics suiting a certain kind of production. It turned up on the soundtrack for 1998's *Phoenix* (specifically the 'Germicide Mix' from the 1994 *Disinfected* EP), a corrupt cop movie starring Ray Liotta, and in the second episode of *Black Bird*, a Dennis Lehane-created crime drama mini-series from 2022 starring Taron Edgerton.

'This Is The Night' 3:50

The title suggests a follow-up to 'This Is The Day', but 'This Is The Night' proves to be its own thing, more closely related to 'Out Of The Blue (Into The Fire)'. Opening with a neat piano riff (the liner notes credit Collard with 'Honky tonk piano'), it soon expands into something darker, where the lust explored in 'Dogs Of Lust' proves all conquering but also somewhat futile. This track went through various iterations, none of them satisfying Johnson, until he stripped it down and reconstructed it by playing its basics on the family's old Bell piano, which had once occupied pride of place in his father's pub. Johnson had relocated the old bar piano (now painted pink) to The Garden studio, a reminder of his roots and the origins of his songwriting. Collard played his section on this 'honky tonk piano', capturing it in a single take (a quick, down-and-dirty approach to recording pervades *Dusk*). Marr added his guitar solo one evening in Johnson's flat, again recorded in one. 'I was fully expecting to do it over and over,' Marr told Johnson's biographer Neil Fraser, 'but he insisted that was it.' The pair then moved on to record a basic take on 'Lung Shadows'. Joining Johnson, Collard and Marr were guest musicians Danny Thompson on acoustic guitar and Bruce Smith on drums.

'This Is The Night' is a conflicted song full of longing and fear. The male subject is 'scared of the things I think of/When night comes along', while expressing a concern with how men treat the women in their lives: 'Oh, it's a wicked world/Awaits the ones our young girls bear'. The middle, darker turn goes back to the notion of one-night stands offering immediate relief, but little in the way of true satisfaction: 'How many whores have walked through that door/Lain by my side and climbed in my mind'. There's a lament for the lost innocence of the past: 'Makes me reach out and weep/For the days when I was pure of heart and/Slept in peace'. The song plays out the promise and threat that lies 'In the fading light of this coming night'.

'Slow Emotion Replay' 3:55

Side one of *Dusk* closes with one of The The's finest tracks, a stand-out on an album full of great songs. Released as the second single (backed with a trio of 'Dogs Of Lust' remixes by J. G. Thirlwell), 'Slow Emotion Replay' spent three weeks in the UK Singles Chart between April and May 1993, reaching a high of number 35.

The song sounds like a riposte to all Johnson's critics, particularly those in the British music press who dismissed him as a bed-sit depressive, forever writing about personal angst and global anxieties. Along with much of *Dusk*, 'Slow Emotion Replay' is a less complex track than most of *Infected* and *Mind Bomb*, so perhaps Johnson was subconsciously responding to those frequent accusations of bombast and grandstanding. Eller was back on bass guitar, with Palmer on drums, but the bulk of the track is the by-play between Johnson on vocals and electric guitar and Marr on electric guitar and harmonica.

The opening verses suggest a level of deep self-reflection, with Johnson looking back on his past work and concluding that he's not so sure about some of the statements he'd written from youthful confidence. They also suggest someone with more maturity, more experience and a willingness to admit he doesn't know it all: 'The more I see/The less I know/About all the things I thought/Were wrong or right/And carved in stone'. The central mea culpa comes in a neat summation of all Johnson's lyrical concerns, amid a request to be left alone: 'So, don't ask me about/War, religion, or God/Love, sex, or death'. This new humility is expressed in the catchy but hugely meaningful couplet 'Everybody knows what's going wrong with the world/ But I don't even know what's going on in myself'. As so often with The The, Johnson wraps deep issues in an upbeat tune, even if his lack of faith provides a kicker: 'And we reach out and pray/To a deaf, dumb, and blind God who never explains'. Tim Pope was back for the accompanying music video (featured in *From Dusk 'Til Dawn*), opening with four minutes of bar-room philosophy (few outlets played out the full extract).

Johnson's new-found humility expressed on 'Slow Emotion Replay' found favour with the critics, with *Select* magazine declaring the single to be 'wonderful' and going on to reprimand those who'd critiqued The The previously: 'It must be great to be Johnson now: all the snide twerps who dismissed him as over forever after the great *Mind Bomb* disaster of 1989 are cowering with their copies of *Dusk* and backtracking like madmen.' The song was revised in 2025 as 'Slow Emotion Replayed' (4:08, released on 11 July 2025), recorded in Studio Cineola, London, and featuring Johnson on Omnichord and vocals, Barrie Cadogan on electric guitar and backing vocals, James Eller on bass, with Gillian Glover also providing backing vocals. This languorous, revised version was featured on the set-list for the final leg of the summer 2025 *Ensoulment* tour. The B-side, 'Crow Commotion Displayed' (4:03), is a haunting, electronic-driven deconstruction of the A-side, omitting Eller's bass guitar while foregrounding Glover's atmospheric vocals.

'Helpline Operator' 4:48

Side two of *Dusk* encapsulates the title of the album even more closely than the opening suite of songs; there's an eerie sense of twilight in the soulless city ('I watch the sun go down on London town') that pervades side two, as is evident by their titles. *Dusk*'s second side offers songs that provide a blues-driven, soulful film noir soundtrack to nocturnal adventures in the big city – not all of them fun.

'Helpline Operator' recasts advice telephone helplines – like those offered by the Samaritans – as a relationship helpline (or even one of those phone sex lines that were all-pervasive in the 1990s). The song casts the singer as the operator taking the calls of 'the lost and the lonely', he's the 'intimate stranger' who offers his ear and in turn takes on their burdens ('Your problems will be mine').

Eller cites this as his favourite track, so it is no surprise that his bassline proves to be the throbbing centre of the song. Unlike several of the *Dusk* tracks, producer Bruce Lampcov took his time, working to get the most suitable sounds out of Eller. They spent as long as it took, reworking the bass line until everyone was happy.

It's an intimate track, with Johnson whispering into the listener's ear. He makes a very specific topic – a telephone helpline – into a universal concern, turning 'Helpline Operator' into another in a long line of The The's frustrated love songs.

'Sodium Light Baby' 3:45

The theme of night and the city continues in 'Sodium Light Baby', in which further frustrated romance/lust pursues the anonymous singer: 'As I sat in the back of that old taxi cab/Waitin' for the evenin' to come/On every street of this city/I hear you call my name'. Whether the sodium lights are those of London or New York, the existential feeling is the same. Johnson admitted that in the early 1990s, the night was his domain, with him rising at three or four in the morning to take long, lonely drives through the deserted city of London. He'd pass the time listening to his own demos – many on *Dusk* – living out the life he was writing about. 'I'd often drive along the empty Embankment,' said Johnson, 'and spent much time wandering around St. Paul's Cathedral and the empty back streets there. [It] helped bring the entire album into focus.'

The song suggests love as an abstract obsession, with attachments to different people at different times provoking varying feelings. In the case here, this unobtainable object of desire is expressed as 'the strangest feelin' I ever had', one that pursues the singer through the city at night under the sodium lights ('And though I ride this city/I can't escape from you'). There's a return to the unfulfilled desires of 'True Happiness This Way Lies' and the unexpressed feelings of 'Love Is Stronger Than Death' in the lines: 'From the day that we are born/To the day that we die/We are hostage to our heart's desire'. Marr's expressive 'wah-wah' guitar underlies the thoughts Johnson is expressing, playing up the sleaze factor of his nocturnal expeditions (and emissions). Love and lust, romance and sex cannot be escaped, no matter how far we run: 'And when I look up to the stars I wonder/Can the world be so cruel?' It can – and Johnson and co are here to chronicle it in all its despair and beauty.

'Lung Shadows' 4:34

Things slow down and take a quieter turn with the doodle that is 'Lung Shadows'. Lyrically light – the couplet 'I close my eyes and you are with me/I can feel your breath upon my body' is all there is – the song nonetheless manages to expand into a four-and-a-half-minute epic of would-be film soundtrack music built around a simple tune. Collard's original French horn instrumentation was replaced by a muted trumpet, with his brass arrangement played by David Lawrence, Chris Batchelor and Ashley Slater. There's a whispered intimacy here, whether real or imagined, whether in the back of that cab from 'Sodium Light Baby' or back home at the conclusion of the night's adventures. It's about atmosphere, introduced by a series of telephone voices (source unknown, as the official liner note credit says), the whispering satellites of 'The Beat(en) Generation' and 'Good Morning Beautiful' from *Mind Bomb* returning. The mood music unfolds for a good while before the slight, huskily-delivered lyrics finally slide in. The repeated line 'Come closer to me' that runs through the remainder is a further expression of The The's forever frustrated romance...

'Bluer Than Midnight' 3:43

There's a similar atmosphere to 'Bluer Than Midnight', another city song (with accompanying street sirens) of sex and dissatisfaction, echoing 'August & September', 'Beyond Love' and – especially – 'Gravitate To Me'. Once more, sin is tempting and irresistible, no matter the effort made: 'One sin leads to another one/Oh, the harder I try/I can never, never, never find peace in this life'. It's a late night exploration of bodily desire, with the opening verse setting the scene: 'The candle are lit, the curtains are drawn/There's still no sign of rain nor dawn/Our lips touch, our limbs entwine/But the ghosts that haunt me won't leave my mind'. Collard provided another skilled piano line (captured in a single take), with Guy Barker providing the evocative trumpet and Vinni Colaiuta on drums. Johnson's vocals end up self-questioning: 'I ask myself/ Where does lust come from/Is it something to yield to or be overcome?' The challenge is one that will always fail, with Johnson offering a bleak conclusion – 'Why can't love ever touch my heart like fear does?' – in stark response to the more optimistic take offered in 'Love Is Stronger Than Death'.

'Lonely Planet' 5:27

Dusk concludes with a cut of perfect upbeat pop. After railing against the world and all its ills for several albums, Johnson had concluded that his outcry had effected little change. He found the answer in a quote from Tolstoy: 'Everyone thinks of changing the world, but no one thinks of changing himself'. It sparked a lyric that became central to 'Lonely Planet', a song that connects the personal with the fate of the world. Green issues, such as climate change – dubbed 'global warming' then – had ever more prominence, so it was inevitable they would creep into Johnson's songwriting.

It's alluded to throughout the track, from the opening line ('Planet Earth is slowing down') through to a simple acknowledgement of overpopulation ('[We're] Running out of space/For the human race'). Throughout, Johnson uses a version of Tolstoy's words as a chorus line – 'If you can't change your world, change yourself' – until the penultimate verse when he reverses the line: 'And if you can't change yourself/Then change the world'. With backing vocals from Zeke Manyika and Paul Webb, Johnson takes a further step in the final section, producing a lament for everything and everyone lost to time, working in those unexpressed feelings often repressed: 'I can't stop thinking of/All the people I've ever loved/All the people I have lost/All the people I'll never know/All the feelings I've never shown'. For a man only in his 30s, it's an expression of a premature nostalgia for a world he fears he's losing, whether personally or in terms of threats to the planet.

Dusk grew out of grief, yet it concludes with a joyous expression of love for the planet and everyone on it ('I'm in love with the planet I'm standing on') culminating in a fear that there's not enough time to do what needs to be done ('The world's too big and life's too short'). Given the inertia and inability to work that overcame Johnson in the early years of the 21st century, this recognition of the shortness of time available in the average human lifespan takes on a new irony.

Related Tracks
'Scenes From Arctic Twilight' 8:52
Consisting of five sections – 'Ancient Lights', 'Wounded', 'Balloon', 'Unseasonable Weather' and 'Arctic Twilight' – this pseudo-film music suite was featured as the B-side tracks for the single release of 'Slow Emotion Replay'. The tunes are early takes on the approach Johnson would take to such soundtracks as *Tony*, *Moonbug* and *Hyena*.

'Darkness Falls' 3:51
Created for the soundtrack of the 1995 movie *Judge Dredd* (based on the signature character from the UK's *2000AD* comic), 'Darkness Falls' is a relatively inconsequential track that Johnson was never too happy with (understandably, with fairy tale lyrics at the beginning ['Mirror, mirror, on the wall'] and threats of a coming storm). The bands involved in the soundtrack were more edgy than the film could ever aspire to, with Johnson alongside The Cure ('Dredd Song'), White Zombie ('Super-Charger Heaven'), Leftfield ('Release The Pressure') and Cocteau Twins ('Need-Fire').

Disinfected EP (1994)
'That Was The Day' 4:01
Released in January 1994, the *Disinfected* EP (co-produced by Johnson and Bruce Lampcov) reached number 17 on the UK Singles Chart (the highest chart position any The The single had reached to that point), staying in the

chart for four weeks. It outperformed every The The single released since (including 'The Beat(en) Generation' – which had topped out at number 18). The EP opened with the re-titled 'That Was The Day', a lighter, laid back version of 'This Is The Day' recorded live at the War Room with Jim Fitting on harmonica and Collard on the Hammond organ and Omnichord.

'Dis-Infected' 5:27

The second track on the *Disinfected* EP was another reworking of an older song – this time 'Infected' – also recorded 'as live' at the War Room. Like 'That Was The Day', the re-titled 'Dis-Infected' lacks some of the punch of the original, but offers a valid, more languid and deliberately paced alternative take on one of The The's defining songs. It shows a band willing to play fast and loose with some of their own established catalogue – some might see this version as the definitive take.

'Helpline Operator (Sick Boy Mix)' 5:02

A remixed version of the track from *Dusk*.

'Dogs Of Lust (Germicide Mix)' 3:09

J. G. Thirlwell's remix of 'Dogs Of Lust'.

Solitude EP (1994)

Released as a nine-track 'album' for the US market, *Solitude* combined the UK *Shades Of Blue* EP [see *Mind Bomb*] with the UK *Disinfected* EP, with an additional track, the remix of 'Violence Of Truth' from *Mind Bomb*.

Hanky Panky (1995)

Personnel:
Matt Johnson: vocals, guitar, bass
Eric Schermerhorn: electric and slide guitar
Gail Ann Dorsey: bass
'Reverend' Brian McLeod: drums
'Gentleman' Jim Fitting: harmonica
D. C. Collard: treated melodica, arrangements
Recorded at The War Room, Pittsburgh, between spring and summer 1994
Producers: Matt Johnson, Bruce Lampcov
Label: 550 Music/Epic
Release date: 14 February 1995 (UK)
Charts: UK: 28
Running time: 41:02
All tracks written by Hank Williams; arrangements/re-arrangements by Matt Johnson and D. C. Collard

Both the *Disinfected* EP and the American compilation *Solitude* marked the end of one phase of Matt Johnson's musical adventures. The re-recording of older tracks and the repackaging of earlier material provided a pause for him to consider his future. Johnson had grown tired of the UK and writing lyrics railing against the seemingly endless Conservative governments. Returning for the *Jingle Hell* tour at the end of 1993 only served to confirm his detachment from his homeland. His relationship with Fiona Skinner finally came to a definitive end, too. She directed the video for the re-done 'That Was The Day' at Alcatraz Island, just off the coast of San Francisco – the video, which featured images from Johnson's childhood and their time together, served as an apt conclusion to their relationship. Although Skinner would no longer be involved with Johnson or The The, her distinctive logotype continued to be used.

America was calling Johnson and he relocated to live in New York. It was to be a fresh start, both personally and professionally. He was keen to immerse himself in the homeland of the blues. During the tour promoting *Dusk*, Johnson had mused about possibly creating a pair of EPs featuring covers of his favourite songs by American blues musicians Robert Johnson and Hank Williams. He saw an opportunity to both pay tribute to those who'd inspired him and a chance to put his own distinctive The The stamp on the songs (as he'd already done with '(In My) Solitude' and 'The Dolphins'). That would be the 'official' reason for his relocation to America.

Faced with whittling down the material to four or five tracks from each singer-songwriter, Johnson found the task impossible. He decided to focus exclusively on Hank Williams, expanding his plan from an EP to a full album of covers that, he admitted to *Musician* magazine, came from 'the darker side of Hank'. These songs would be in tune with his own songwriting, so the pairing of Williams' songs with Johnson's musical approach was the perfect fit. Johnson had already recruited D. C. Collard during the *Dusk* tour, and the pair reunited at Johnson's holiday home in Spain in 1994 to rework Hank Williams. They were later joined by American guitarist Eric Schermerhorn, who'd previously been working with Iggy Pop and David Bowie. Initially, Schermerhorn had reservations about an English musician covering the 'sacred ground' of American country/folk music. Meeting Johnson and familiarising himself with his back catalogue soon put his mind at rest.

The trio reunited at the War Room studio in Pittsburgh for the recording of *Hanky Panky*, working first on 'Honky Tonkin''. Bruce Lampcov was co-producing, and he and Johnson adopted the latest technological innovations, including the then-new Pro Tools software. Talking to New York magazine *The Island Ear*, Johnson explained his approach. 'We initially put the songs down in the same tempo, structure and key as Hank. I would sing them exactly as Hank sang them. Then, I decided to change the key to suit me, and I changed the way I sang them. I changed the music around so it changed the atmosphere.' What Johnson was engaged in was adapting Williams' work to the unique style Johnson had developed under his The The banner. The finished project clearly featured Hank Williams' songs, but cleverly reinterpreted in the distinctive style of The The.

Born in 1923 in Alabama, Hiram King Williams – known as Hank – learned to play guitar from African-American blues musician Rufus Payne. After winning an amateur talent contest, Williams' professional career began in the late 1930s, working with a group of musicians known as the Drifting Cowboys. His career progressed in fits and starts, hampered by alcoholism. In 1947, 'Honky Tonkin'' led to a recording contract with MGM Records and a regular slot on radio show *The Grand Ole Opry*. A series of hits followed, including 'Your Cheatin' Heart', 'Hey Good Looking' and 'I'm So Lonesome I Could Cry'. Married, divorced and re-married, Williams' life was chaotic, and his alcoholism cost him the *Grand Ole Opry* gig due to his unreliability. He died suddenly of heart failure, aged 29, while heading to a concert in Ohio on New Year's Day 1953. Williams' biggest success came posthumously, with his work influencing many of the folk and country singers of the 1960s and 1970s, including Johnny Cash, Elvis Presley, Bob Dylan and The Rolling Stones. Multiple awards followed, culminating in a Pulitzer Prize Special Citation in 2010 for his 'craftsmanship as a songwriter who expressed universal feelings with poignant simplicity.'

Talking to Wesley Doyle in 2024, Johnson looked back at *Hanky Panky* with affection. 'In my mind, it seemed a natural thing to do. Yes, I'm a musician, a producer, a singer, but if I had to choose just one term, it would be songwriter. That's what I think I'm best at and what I love doing. I'm fascinated by the tradition of songwriting and how it evolved, how certain elements originated in England, Europe and Africa as well.'

Making *Hanky Panky* allowed Johnson to shake off his habits and tendency to procrastinate (although a covers album could be seen as a form of procrastination, delaying any further original material). The album came out just two years after *Dusk* and was prepared and recorded across just three months in 1994. Johnson contributed lightly in terms of playing instruments. *Hanky Panky* was a musical holiday, a chance to be a singer, interpreting someone else's work, free from the pressure to create. Talking to *Uncut*, Johnson mused: 'I just wanted to get inside another songwriter's songs. *Dusk* was quite a hard record to write, but I wanted to keep working. There were a lot of raised eyebrows at the label...'

While Sony in the US understood what Johnson was striving to do, in the UK, it was a different story. The market was very different, and the label didn't see a place for *Hanky Panky* during the early days of 'Britpop'. The album only hit the UK Album Chart for two weeks, reaching number 28 on its week of release. The sales were low and the critical reaction was muted. Andy Gill, writing in *The Independent*, suggested Johnson had made a misstep: 'Mostly, *Hanky Panky* demonstrates a misapprehension of Williams' art, the greatness of which lies, in part, in his ability to disguise darkness and loneliness in redemptively light settings.' For *The Observer*, it was Johnson's transformation of Williams' songs into his own idiom that was the problem: 'Gloomy rock replaces the original relaxed melodies, and Johnson's baritone evokes only one colour from Hank's mixed palette of emotions.'

Johnson took solace from the fact that *Hanky Panky* was more critically successful in his new home. 'It got fantastic reviews in America', he told *Uncut*. 'Hank's daughter wrote me a lovely letter saying, 'My daddy would be proud of what you've done." Colin Escott, Hank Williams' biographer, felt that Johnson provided the finest covers of Williams' work to that point. North American critical reaction was much more upbeat compared to British critics. *The Calgary Herald* noted that 'it's taken a Brit to unearth the spirit, the soul, the songs of Hank Williams', while *Entertainment Weekly* maintained that 'Johnson internalises Williams' '50s despair and coughs it up as modernist melancholy.' New York's *Trouser Press* hailed *Hanky Panky* as 'a tour-de-force tribute' that 'might have sunk to self-conscious gimmickry in less perceptive hands, but Johnson makes it work beautifully.' For *The Chicago Tribune*, Johnson's take on Williams 'drones with the over-miked rasp, sometimes monotonous echo, and bluesy guitars that are The The's trademark.'

'Honky Tonkin'' 3:36

With most tracks coming in well under four minutes, *Hanky Panky* packs in 11 songs, where most previous albums included around eight. In this respect, Johnson's versions closely follow the Hank Williams originals, which are mostly under three minutes. Where he deviates is in the more ferocious rhythm of the songs – in keeping with The The's musical attitude. For all their melancholy content, the originals tend to be more laid back. 'Honky Tonkin'' kicks off with a relaxed country-style guitar riff that quickly gives way to a more pounding, grinding rhythm, with Schermerhorn on slide guitar. Johnson,

Lampcov and engineer Nick Hunt provide the accompanying tambourines. It's unmistakably by The The, with even Williams' lyrics lending themselves to Johnson's sensibilities. The instrumental break/fade out broadens the atmospheric sounds, playing into the late-night city atmosphere evoked by *Dusk*. In liner notes, Johnson wrote: 'While the band and I have attempted to The The-ise [Williams'] music, and stretch and twist it around a bit, we've also tried to stay true to the emotional essence...'

The song was originally a B-side to Williams' May 1948 single 'Pan American'. The more vibrant MGM Records version was recorded in Nashville on 6 November 1947. Matt Johnson further adapted the tune to match his own sensibilities, while the lyrics must have felt as though they were written for him: 'When you're sad and lonely/And have no place to go/Come to see me baby/And bring along some dough'.

'Six More Miles' 0:57
The original Hank Williams version of 'Six More Miles' was a B-side to the September 1948 release of 'I Saw The Light'. It was one of Williams' earliest compositions, first published in 1945. Williams recorded it (under the full title 'Six More Miles (To The Graveyard)') in April 1947, but it wasn't released until 'I Saw The Light' came out 18 months later. This song was literally the flip side to 'I Saw The Light', rejecting any sense of salvation and dropping the upbeat tempo. It's the story of a disconsolate man travelling to the graveyard to bury his lover, an example of 'Gothic country'. Johnson strips the track right back to the basics with his simple vocal take accompanied only by Collard's harmonium – the finished piece clocks in at under a minute. It provides a brief break between the faster-paced, more upbeat 'Honky Tonkin'' and 'My Heart Would Know'.

'My Heart Would Know' 3:32
The first track on *Hanky Panky* to feature the full band (and the first with drums), 'My Heart Would Know' was a late Hank Williams track, released on 22 June 1951. It was the B-side to 'Hey Good Lookin'', recorded in Nashville on 16 March 1951 with members of the Drifting Cowboys. The well-composed lyrics are simple, a cry from the heart by a narrator who's still in love with an ex-partner who no longer loves him: 'My lips could tell a lie/But my heart would know'. Joining Johnson were Schermerhorn on acoustic and electric guitars (he makes his presence felt in the instrumental breaks), Collard on Hammond organ, Brian MacLeod on drums and Gail Ann Dorsey on bass guitar, billed as 'Hollywood' Dorsey.

Born in 1962 in Pennsylvania, Dorsey had a long career as a session player, working with David Bowie between 1995 and his final tour in 2004. She worked and performed in London in the 1980s at the same time Johnson was first making his mark. While working with Johnson on *Hanky Panky*, she joined Tears For Fears, writing, recording and touring with the band between

1993 and 1996. Dorsey played with The The for a few live television appearances promoting *Hanky Panky* in the UK and the US.

'If You'll Be A Baby To Me' 0:59
Another interstitial at just under a minute, 'If You'll Be A Baby To Me' reverts to just Collard on harmonium and piano and Johnson on vocals. The original lyrics are intact, even if the references to the wife 'keeping the home fires burning' while the man does the ploughing and milking seem somewhat dated. The song dates from 1952, but it wasn't afforded a proper release until the summer of 1961, almost a decade after Williams' death. For his version, Johnson keeps things simple, short and sweet, providing a neat buffer between the first few numbers and offering a sampling of the range of Hank Williams' material. As Johnson wrote, he didn't choose the obvious songs to cover. 'The choice of songs here may, or may not, surprise people, but after many months of both listening to virtually everything he ever recorded and reading every published lyric I could find, I decided to follow my instinct and interpret the ones that moved me the most on a raw, emotional level.'

'I'm A Long Gone Daddy' 4:41
Hank Williams recorded 'I'm A Long Gone Daddy' in 1948, with the track becoming his second top-ten hit (after 1947's 'Move It On Over' reached the top five). It would set the formula for much of Williams' work, consisting of an upbeat honky-tonk take with a bluesy edge. That recording session also produced the familiar second version of 'Honky Tonkin'' and 'I Can't Get You Off Of My Mind', among others. Johnson stretches the original 2:59 recording to 4:41, making it a The The-style full-band epic. Opening with Johnson's vocal alone ('All you want to do is sit around and pout/And now I got enough, so I'm getting out'), things kick into a higher gear with The The trademark 'wah wah' electric guitar from Schermerhorn and Johnson, with Dorsey on bass guitar. Fitting delivers the harmonica line towards the end, while Collard operates the sounds from the 'treated' melodica. The sentiments of the song, about a disintegrating relationship, echo any number of previous The The tracks, as does the instrumental break that could have come from almost any track on *Dusk*.

'Weary Blues From Waitin'' 2:47
A late Williams track, 'Weary Blues From Waitin'' was released in September 1953, nine months after his unexpected death. The song was recorded as a demo in 1951, but in the wake of Williams' early death, there was new demand for his material. MGM called in the Drifting Cowboys to provide new overdubs. Upon release, the single reached number seven on the country chart, providing an early indication that the Hank Williams legend would only grow. This version from The The features just two performers, Johnson on vocals and Schermerhorn on acoustic guitar, delivering a simple rendition of a

typical heart-rending Williams composition. It's the most straightforwardly country-sounding track on *Hanky Panky*, stripped of virtually all The The touches. The subject ('These blues have got me cryin") goes right to the heart of the musical project Johnson had been pursuing for over a decade. He turns on the melancholy on the lines: 'Through tears I watch young lovers/As they go strolling by/For all the things that might have been/God forgive me if I cry'. This track was one of four (the others being 'Honky Tonkin", 'I Saw The Light' and 'I'm A Long Gone Daddy') issued as a promotional EP under the title *Four Play (Some Hanky Panky)* in 1994.

'I Saw The Light' 2:38

The only single from *Hanky Panky*, 'I Saw The Light' is an unmistakable The The track. Regarded as 'country gospel', it had been inspired by a phrase used by Williams' mother (who, along with his first wife Audrey Sheppard, managed his career). Released in September 1948 – the first track Williams recorded under his new deal with MGM Records – the song did not enjoy significant success. It was only much later that it became the centrepiece of the Hank Williams songbook. Williams drew upon lines from the Bible for inspiration, causing his biographer Colin Escott to note that 'I Saw The Light' was 'the prayer of the backslider, who lives in hope of redemption'. Little wonder that Johnson felt it was a suitable single. It became a country and gospel standard, covered by many and used as the title of the 2015 Hank Williams biopic starring Tom Hiddleston. The The performed the song on an instalment of *Beavis And Butt-Head* in 1995.

'I Saw The Light' boasts a spectacular music video. Inspired by photojournalist Margaret Bourke-White's 1929 images of the top of the then-recently completed Chrysler Building in New York, Johnson decided to feature the giant silver modernist gargoyles. Working with director Samuel Bayer, Johnson concocted a scenario that saw him and a band perform atop the Chrysler Building, with the intrepid singer venturing out on top of the bird-like silver protrusion, high above the New York skyline. Johnson couldn't get insured to do the stunt himself, so an actual stuntman was required. In a necessary 'cheat', a replica of one of the eagles was built on the flat surface of a neighbouring skyscraper, allowing Johnson to appear to be walking the line high in the sky. The shots were filmed from a circling helicopter piloted by a Vietnam War veteran who held a license allowing him to fly closer to New York's buildings, with the production explaining to the building's management that they were filming for a commercial. 'I'd actually sneaked out onto the edge of a gargoyle myself and nearly went over the edge, it was so cold and slippery', Johnson recalled.

'Your Cheatin' Heart' 3:43

Hank Williams' signature, 'Your Cheatin' Heart' was recorded in September 1952 and released the following January. It came at a time when Williams' career was going through a purple patch with multiple hits. At the same time, his private life was in turmoil with his first marriage to Audrey Sheppard falling apart. He was also battling alcoholism and addiction to painkillers and morphine (the result of a failed operation for back pain). After his divorce, Williams was dating his soon-to-be second wife, Billie Jean Jones. Travelling to meet with her parents, Williams discussed his past and described his first wife as a 'cheatin' heart'. Momentarily inspired, he dictated the lyrics to Jones. The song was recorded during Williams' last sessions, and he regarded it as among his best. The song came out after Williams' death, selling over a million copies and staying at the top spot of the *Billboard* Country and Western Chart for six weeks. 'Your Cheatin' Heart' became synonymous with the short life of Hank Williams, providing the title for the 1964 biopic that starred George Hamilton and for the 1990 John Byrne-scripted Scottish television drama starring Tilda Swinton (several Hank Williams tracks featured on the soundtrack). Johnson's version opens with Collard's distinctive 'honky tonk' piano, now a firm fixture of the sound of The The. Fitting was back on harmonica, MacLeod on drums and Dorsey on bass, with Schermerhorn taking the (occasionally distorted) lead guitar, freeing Johnson to focus solely on his vocal delivery.

'I Can't Get You Off Of My Mind' 2:58
The full band were back again for this, a Williams track from the 1940s that featured as the B-side to the single 'A Mansion On The Hill'. Recorded in November 1947, the song (released over a year later in December 1948) saw the narrator lament his love for his unfaithful partner. The subject matter and lyrics must have appealed to Johnson as something he could have written himself back in the 1980s. Johnson joined Schermerhorn on guitar, with the latter playing acoustic and slide guitar. Collard's organ and Harmonium are pressed into service alongside Fitting's harmonica. Dorsey on bass and MacLeod on drums fill out the full band sound. The muscular guitars pop up between verses before Johnson's vocal is accompanied by a simple acoustic guitar. Refusing to outstay its welcome, 'I Can't Get You Off Of My Mind' ultimately drifts off in a musical jam.

'There's A Tear In My Beer' 3:22
Starting very simply, Johnson's take builds slowly as various instruments join in. Williams' original from 1951 fell on stony ground as his producer, Fred Rose, did not want to release songs featuring alcohol. The song was passed on to Big Bill Lister (who often opened for Williams on the road) when he made it known to Williams that he needed 'a drinking song' for his own shows. Lister released the song in 1952 on Capitol. In 1988, Williams' son – Hank Williams Jr, also a singer-songwriter – used technology to create a 'duet' with his father's recording, merging their vocals. Father and son were awarded a Grammy in 1988. Johnson took the simple approach, although the

musicality builds as each band member joins in. As the piece builds in intensity, so does the emotionality, highlighting the way drinking has replaced romance: 'There's a tear in my beer/Cause I'm crying for you dear/You are on my lonely mind'.

'I Can't Escape From You' 4:16
The *Hanky Panky* closer is one of the longer tracks at over four minutes, alongside 'I'm A Long Gone Daddy'. The song originated as another Hank Williams demo from 1951, released posthumously. Like 'Weary Blues From Waitin'', it was augmented by overdubs from the Drifting Cowboys and released in September 1953. It's another tale of a man haunted by the memory of a lost love, one unlamented, where the narrator had been 'a slave to a heart of stone'. Although the original was just Williams singing while playing guitar (the same way Johnson and Schermerhorn tackled 'Weary Blues From Waitin''), this time, Johnson adds Collard's harmonium and piano and Fitting's harmonica, giving it a more overall The The sound. There's something of the church testimonial about Collard's playing and Fitting's warbling harmonica. The lyrics once again must have struck Johnson as familiar, an echo of his own 'Sodium Light Baby' on *Dusk*; compare Williams' 'But wherever I go I always know/I can't escape from you' to Johnson's 'And though I ride this city/I can't escape from you'. It shows how aligned both Williams' and Johnson's sensibilities were, and clearly reveals Johnson's own debt to the work of Williams and Robert Johnson. Fittingly, the track ends with a vocal extract of Williams signing off, lifted from the 1993 compilation album *Hank Williams: Health And Happiness Shows*. Johnson provided liner notes for the 1995 compilation of Hank Williams demos, *Alone And Forsaken*.

Related Tracks
'I'm Free At Last' 2:36
One of a trio of additional Hank Williams covers released on the CD single of 'I Saw The Light', 'I'm Free At Last' is a simple vocal and acoustic guitar combination in which the narrator laments his freedom from love.

'Someday You'll Call My Name' 2:39
This second additional track is an equally simple take on Williams' posthumously released song.

'There's No Room In My Heart For The Blues' 2:50
Completing the trio of extras on the 'I Saw The Light' CD single, this version comes complete with Matt Johnson's false start, studio talk back and a second take, providing more of a vocal workout.

Naked Self (2000)

Personnel:
Matt Johnson: vocals, electric guitar, acoustic guitar, baritone guitar, bass guitar, banjo
Eric Schermerhorn: electric guitar, acoustic guitar, baritone guitar, bass guitar
Spencer Campbell: bass guitar (on 'Boiling Point', 'Shrunken Man', 'The Whisperers' and 'Weather Belle')
Earl Harvin: drums (on 'Boiling Point', 'Shrunken Man', 'The Whisperers', 'Global Eyes', 'Swine Fever' and 'Weather Belle')
Brian MacLeod: drums (on 'Voidy Numbness')
Frank Ferrer: drums (on 'Salt Water')
Dorit Chrysler, Michelle Amar, Lloyd Cole, Brian Kelley: backing vocals (on 'Global Eyes')
Recorded at Sear Sound, Harold Dessau Studios, New York, between 1999 and 2000
Producers: Matt Johnson, Bruce Lampcov
Label: Nothing/Universal
Release date: 29 February 2000 (UK)
Charts: UK: 45, Aus: 127, Ger: 80
Running time: 45:38
All tracks written by Matt Johnson, except where stated

Having exorcised his obsession with the American blues, Matt Johnson's next step was to take up residence in the US. In a way, he was simply joining his *Hanky Panky* bandmates – D. C. Collard had already moved to New York, and Eric Schermerhorn lived there, too. If Johnson was going to produce more music with this incarnation of The The, it made sense for him to be based in the Big Apple. Renting out his London flat and handing over management of his recording studio, The Garden, Johnson packed his bags, left the 51st state and flew to New York.

There was another, more personal reason: romance. Johnson had met Swedish model and actress Johanna St Michaels in Los Angeles several years before his move. In a 'showbiz' cliché, they'd met at a pool party in the Hollywood Hills. Johnson invited St Michaels to his next concert, which she professed to be 'blown away' by. The relationship continued after Johnson returned to London. Whenever in LA, Johnson would hook up with St Michaels, with the pair staying in the notorious Chateau Marmont. Further meetings followed in New York, Stockholm and London as their relationship deepened. Talking to Neil Fraser, Johnson confirmed: 'I moved to New York simply because Johanna and I had fallen in love. It was a completely natural move for me as I already had a lot of friends there and I knew the city inside out.'

Shortly after relocating, Johnson re-connected with Collard and spent time in New York studios working on the later abandoned *Gun Sluts*. For several weeks at Sear Sound on West 48th Street, Collard and Johnson created a 'very experimental' work, utilising unconventional instruments like the Theremin, alongside other instruments Johnson favoured, like the Hammond organ. Eric Schermerhorn joined alongside newcomer Earl Harvin on drums. Johnson also brought in bass guitarist Spencer Campbell.

Johnson found himself working closer with Schermerhorn – the pair lived near each other. That resulted in them co-writing, something Johnson had largely avoided. As a result, the songs became more guitar-based, so Johnson dispensed with keyboards altogether, resulting in the departure of Collard. By 1996, the pair were at Harold Dessau studios, having decided that the Sear Sound sessions had not been productive.

Gun Sluts would quickly join *Spirits* and *The Pornography Of Despair* as another legendary lost album. Johnson was still working with Sony, but his latest project ran into a problem. 'They hated *Gun Sluts*', Johnson told *Uncut*. 'It was my version of [Lou Reed's] *Metal Machine Music*. I wasn't doing it to break the contract. It's just where I was at the time, going in some interesting new directions, listening to experimental music.' Unusually, Johnson had approached *Gun Sluts* by creating the music first, leaving the lyrics until later (the project was abandoned before any songs could be completed; some would feed into *Naked Self* like 'Diesel Breeze', while the track 'Gun Sluts' would be released as a single sold on tour).

Perhaps Johnson felt some difficulty in writing lyrics again following *Hanky Panky* and having been so immersed in the world of Hank Williams. *Gun Sluts* was a move in the opposite direction, with lengthy instrumental noise-driven tracks, some stretching over 15 minutes. This was not what Sony expected. Talking to the *Phoenix New Times* in May 2000, Johnson admitted: 'We made this really unstructured, aggressive recording, a really great album. Sony were horrified. They were like, 'Either change this or we can't use it.' So, I shelved the album...'

Having dropped *Gun Sluts*, Johnson decided to write and produce a more traditional The The album, hoping it would be a more commercial prospect for Sony. 'When it was finished, my contract with Sony was finally up after 17 years', said Johnson. 'I played them *Naked Self*, and they didn't like that, either. They asked me if I could make it more commercial, and I was outraged. I said, 'Forget it.'' That was just the prelude to a legal battle between Johnson and Sony that lasted over a year as he tried to free himself from the contract while retaining ownership of *Naked Self*. Johnson told *Uncut* he didn't particularly want to quit Sony: 'I was happy to stay, but I wanted a proper contract. They said, 'We just don't see big hits.' I was quite upset, but they were right because there weren't any big hits on it.'

Johnson found it difficult to focus on *Naked Self*, given the distractions of New York. His work ethic diminished; gone was the full concentration of his early recordings or the intense focus required for *Infected*. Without a record label, Johnson abandoned work in favour of fun. A brief relocation to Spain failed to make Johnson and Schermerhorn more productive. Johnson was also continuing his evolution as an autodidact, reading widely, especially Eastern philosophy, Noam Chomsky and other intellectuals. He still didn't find it any easier to write the lyrics that had eluded him since 1993. 'He could get sidetracked really easily', said Schermerhorn of Johnson.

One major distraction was the birth of Johnson and St Michael's first child, Jackson, in May 1997 in Greenwich Village. Coincidentally, Schermerhorn also became a father around this time, further bonding the collaborators. They discovered they worked on material differently: Schermerhorn worked at a faster pace, while Johnson indulged in long, drawn-out meditation, working over a single phrase until he was happy. Johnson often used fridge magnets to compose lyrics or titles, spending hours working through this domestic Burroughs' 'cut-ups' technique. Later, he'd type up the lyrics using his outmoded Remington Rand Model One typewriter. Half the tracks on *Naked Self* would be co-writes with his guitarist.

Johnson decided to use analogue recording gear and instruments, opting for a raw approach, a move back to his teenage years at DeWolfe. The absence of keyboards and the focus on guitar gave *Naked Self* a subtly different sound. Concerned that some might conclude he'd made a 'bad' record – in terms of recording technique – Johnson placed a disclaimer on the sleeve: 'Due to the age and nature of the equipment used in this recording, minor distortions and discrepancies may be detectable.' The delays, false starts and distractions meant that *Naked Self* took the better part of four years, from 1996 to 2000. Drummer Earl Harvin and Kenny Rogers' bassist Spencer Campbell (replacing Gail Ann Dorsey, who'd returned to work with David Bowie) came and went as needed.

After splitting from Sony, Johnson had signed with Nothing Records, an imprint of Interscope, for *Naked Self*. He felt comfortable on a more independent outfit. However, by 1996, Interscope had been absorbed by Seagram and Universal Music Group and merged with PolyGram, A&M and Geffen Records to form a larger conglomerate. Amid the corporate restructuring, there were mass layoffs. When it came time to release and promote *Naked Self*, Johnson found himself dealing with a label that had lost interest. Very little was done to promote the album, even down to failing to supply review copies to critics or make Johnson available for promotional interviews.

Talking to *Uncut*, Johnson recalled the turmoil. 'I hated it. There was only one part of Universal that showed any interest, the German outlet – they were fantastic. Strangely, *Naked Self* got the best reviews of any record I ever made! The tour support ran out for a six-month world tour, so I started to pay for it out of my own pocket because I really believed in the album and the band.'

Johnson was right when it came to reviews of *Naked Self*, even if sales were lacklustre. *The Times* said *Naked Self* 'throbs and growls with expressions of deep dissatisfaction, both personal and political. It's a grimy, low-down rock record. A thrillingly gritty and distorted adventure.' *The Independent* agreed: 'Not many other songwriters can dissect both the personal and the political with equal conviction. His lyrics are full of reassurance in the face of loneliness, consumerism and the other evils [of] the modern world.' Even the establishment-focused *Daily Telegraph* said good things: 'conviction and idealism ... shine through his art, imbuing his songs with an almost physical sense of passion.'

For the British music press, *Naked Self* opened some eyes (and ears). For *NME*, Johnson had 'returned from shadows few ever emerge from', while *Q* noted that it featured 'some of Johnson's most impressive songwriting. A frequently beautiful, moving and thought-provoking addition to the The The catalogue.' *Uncut* called *Naked Self* 'compelling, uncompromising and often beautiful music', while *Later* described the album as 'uncompromising and intense ... [It] makes you realise how soft, inoffensive and unpolitical alternative music has become.'

In the US, the reviews were – if anything – even more positive. According to *Rolling Stone*, *Naked Self* 'finds Johnson returning to the slow-burn industrial grind of his best work. Everything on the album is driven by storm-trooping drums, a battalion of distorted axes and Johnson's ominous echo-chamber vocals.' The *Chicago Tribune* was also a fan: 'The pervasive gloom and apocalyptic imagery of Johnson's music has often overshadowed his sly wit and wry sense of humour. *Naked Self*, which could well be his most vicious and visceral release to date, is a modern-day blues album, steeped in distortion and cynical takes on love and loneliness. Johnson makes clear that even though mass success has generally passed him by, he's more than happy to have done things his own iconoclastic way.' *Flaunt* magazine hailed *Naked Self* as 'the loosest, most aggressive-sounding record that has ever carried the moniker of The The. Stripped down musically, guitars dominate ... most of the songs sport dark, ominous atmospherics. What remains are the deeply personal and introspective lyrics, which, through the years, have revealed a man whose cynicism and optimism create a constant inner struggle.' Few artists could fail to welcome reviews such as these, but it was small compensation for the fact that so few people actually heard the album that took Matt Johnson four years to create. [Note: The titles on *Naked Self* are presented as single words – 'BoilingPoint' – but here they're not, for ease of reading.]

'Boiling Point' (Matt Johnson, Eric Schermerhorn) 5:48

A distant siren (suggesting the twilight city) plays out over brisk drumming that gives way to distorted, reversed guitar before bursting into life with distortion, echoes and twangy guitar riffs against hesitant drums. Soon, the rhythm is in place with Harvin's solid stick work, and the dominant guitar lines give Johnson something to sing against – almost a rap, duetting with his own whispered alter-ego.

The song captures the atmosphere of a late-night train journey, the avoidance of possibly hostile passengers and the fear of loneliness (in the crowded city): 'Don't you ever get lonely/Do you wanna come home with me?' It's grim and grimy, a slice of nocturnal New York or London, capturing the sense of graffitied trains and hostile street people, while holding out the (eternal) hope of connection. There's the continued exploration of disputed meanings, with 'But when is a word/Not a word?/How's the meaning/Been reversed?/Twisted, torn/Tricked and turned/Inside out/Upside down'. Such concerns would flourish in later 21st-century tracks like 'Cognitive Dissident', but they have their beginning here, right at the turn of the millennium.

Canadian outlet *Exclaim!* said that 'Boiling Point' 'rides an intense groove that could have been borrowed from Massive Attack's *Mezzanine*, and it doesn't get much more comfortable after that...'

'Shrunken Man' 4:55

For Johnson, 'Shrunken Man' was a return to the existential self-criticism of *Mind Bomb* and *Dusk*: 'He's just an imperfect man/Trapped in an imperfect body/Ain't happy or sad, lonely or sorry'. 'Boiling Point' crossfades into 'Shrunken Man' as the grinding guitars lead the rumbling, strutting track. Melancholia is to the fore, depicting a sense of paralysis and an inability to cope with the modern world. The second half spins out some optimism from rough raw material: 'But some days in little ways/Love seeps out in the things he says/And all he really wants/Is to feel grown up again'. The old recording equipment comes into its own here, distorting the sounds of the analogue instruments in a way almost impossible to recreate with digital tools. There's something of the central riff of Paul McCartney's *James Bond* theme, 'Live And Let Die', in the relentless, dominant guitars, with Schermerhorn using an old Echoplex tape machine to roughen the guitar sounds.

'The Whisperers' (Johnson, Schermerhorn) 3:20

So much of Johnson's earliest output had been dubbed by the British music press as 'bedsit teenage angst', which to a degree is true. He'd largely written from a male point of view, while being only too happy to explore the shortcomings of his own sex ('The Twilight Hour' on *Soul Mining* being a prime example). As he and his songwriting matured, he introduced a female perspective, especially in his duets with Neneh Cherry on 'Slow Train To Dawn' and Sinead O'Connor on 'Kingdom Of Rain' – these (literally) introduced a female voice. Johnson had rarely written an entire song from a woman's perspective where he attributed to women the same shortcomings in romance, love and lust that he had previously been only too happy to explore in men.

On 'The Whisperers', he writes about a woman waiting for the phone to ring, wondering what her friends really think of her. Has a romantic betrayal resulted in her 'Staying in on Friday night/Lying in her birthday suit'? Johnson adopts his rarely used falsetto, especially in the chorus. Schermerhorn's melodic guitar line that underpins the track keeps things going, while Harvin's drums keep time. The acoustic guitar features in the chorus that introduces a possibly unwanted enlightenment: 'Don't get sad/When people that you trust stab you in the back/So, you thought they were your friends?/Now you know (Now you know)/There's one thing in life that holds/You're on your own (you've gotta grow)'. It's a subtle lament, presented in a crisp song.

'The Whisperers' was issued as a promo-only single but could have been an excellent choice for a proper release. Unfortunately, the lack of promotion put paid to any such notions. Like much of Johnson's work, the downbeat lyrics are coupled with an upbeat musical track, effectively hiding the melancholia of existence in plain sight.

'Soul Catcher' 3:15

One of the best The The cuts of all time, 'Soul Catcher' does exactly what the title suggests. Here, Johnson's self-examination looks to the future and questions his achievements so far. By the release of *Naked Self*, Johnson was in his late 30s, a new father, facing middle age. He captures the sense of time passing and aspirations unachieved in the lines 'But I can't say it/Because I can barely face it/My life is halfway through/And I still haven't done/What I'm here to do'. It was a subject he'd tackled as early as 1983's *Soul Mining* on 'I've Been Waitin' For Tomorrow (All Of My Life)': 'Another year over and what have I done?/All my aspirations have shrivelled in the sun'.

Johnson also anticipates the ennui and stasis that would overcome him for much of the first decade of the 21st century: 'Even though the chances flowed/I sat and watched the hours fold/In upon themselves'. Although he'd make new music, often soundtracks, it would be the better part of a quarter century before Johnson returned to a full album of songs. 'Soul Catcher' pushes regret to the fore, not only for opportunities missed but for future ambitions likely to slip by unachieved. It's elegiac, cutting to the heart of all creatives – will your work ever be completed or be left undone?

It does end on an up note, with the narrator concluding: 'What you give is what you get/And the only thing worth having/Is happiness'. The title came from Johnson's regular trips with his son to the Museum of American Indians, which displayed collections of native American soul catchers.

'Global Eyes' 4:10

While the first four tracks on *Naked Self* dealt with subjects the album title suggested (loneliness, fear, betrayal, angst), with 'Global Eyes' (a witty pun on 'globalise'), things turn political. There's something of Dylan's cue cards from 'Subterranean Homesick Blues' in the rhyming couplets of 'Global Eyes' and something of the vocal approach heard in rap. The anti-capitalist viewpoint is clear from this 'enigmatic anti-star' (per the *AV Club*): 'Mobilise/Globalise/Hypnotise/Homogenise'.

Musically, this features just Johnson on vocals and guitars with Harvin on drums. What really makes it are the slightly out-of-sync backing vocals from Dorit Chrysler, Michelle Amar, Lloyd Cole and Brian Kelly. The inclusion of Cole happened because he was also using the Dessau studio. The Englishmen in New York caught up over a coffee and agreed to contribute to each other's albums. As Cole later wrote (in a 2008 Q&A): 'Matt and I became friends when we were neighbours in a studio complex in Lower Manhattan in the mid to late 1990s, but I was already a fan. We chose Paul Hardiman to produce *Rattlesnakes* [Cole's 1984 debut album, recorded at The Garden] because we all loved the sound of *Soul Mining*.' Johnson returned the favour, contributing vocals to Cole's 'Memphis' (written by actress Karen Black for Robert Altman's 1975 film *Nashville*) on his 2006 *Etc.* album.

Although written in 1997, 'Global Eyes' was more timely upon release in 2000, with protests gathering against neoliberalism and the globalist agenda. The song even anticipates the later 'Occupy' movement(s) of 2011-2016 that protested economic inequality. Talking to *The Aquarian Weekly* in 2000, Johnson said: 'I think we're facing a world of the corporation versus the individual. Corporations are becoming more powerful than entire nations.' In the 25 years since, its concerns have not aged a day, with Johnson's lyrics anticipating the conformity required by society and social media: 'Shut your eyes/Don't criticise/Truth hides in plain sight/Kentucky fried genocide'.

'December Sunlight' (Johnson, Schermerhorn) 3:18

The personal is once more to the fore on this co-write between Johnson and Schermerhorn (also the only two performers). As with 'The Whisperers', Johnson privileges a female character escaping coercive control. It's a simple guitar-and-vocals tune with a sunny aspect: 'She'd read it in her stars/And now she felt it in her heart/That life was gonna start getting better'. Each verse/chorus is punctuated by Schermerhorn's reverberating guitar. It's a vignette of change, an escape from oppression and an openness to positive experience: 'But now she's changing the way she feels/About wasting her time and tears' and 'And she feels alive/And wants to drink every kiss/Make up for what she's missed/And wipe him out of her mind'. Towards the end, Johnson adds self-recrimination, if not about him personally then perhaps about men in general: 'Someday he'll have to grow up/And come clean/And listen to the screams of his own conscience/Cry out, Cry out, Cry out/...And she'll not hear a sound'. Johnson's vocals become ever more emphatic as he reaches this point of self-awareness, putting a downer on an otherwise upbeat and hopeful narrative.

'Swine Fever' 3:39

Johnson's attention turns back to politics and consumerism with the curious 'Swine Fever'. Again, it's a two-hander, Johnson on guitars and vocals with Harvin providing drums. He'd previously criticised the Britain of the 1980s in songs like 'Heartland', but here Johnson was looking further afield, at the all-encompassing global reach of consumerism. In 'Heartland', he'd positioned the UK as the 51st state of the US. Now, at the beginning of the 21st century, the entire world seemed to have been swallowed by American culture. Interviewed by fellow musician Dot Allison, Johnson explained his view: 'Day-to-day life is utterly saturated with advertising. It's hard to get away from it.'

Johnson himself adopts an aggressive stance, emulating the nature of the jingles and ad spots that invade the internet experience in 2025. Overdubbed guitars on a simple riff from Johnson build into a towering sound, dominating the way advertising dominates the public space. The lyrics may be obvious, but they have a straightforward simplicity that makes the message as intrusive as the advertising it criticises. Consumer culture is properly skewered with chorus lines like: 'Don't even like it/But you've just gotta try it/You don't even want it/But you're gonna buy/Gonna-gonna-gonna buy it'. The song ends with a twist, the collapse of capitalism when there's nothing left to own, an implied criticism of the wealthy 1% (even more relevant in the world of Musk and Bezos): 'But what is the point of possessing the world/When you do not even possess yourself?/What is the point of selling your soul/When there's nothing left to buy/And nowhere to go'. A cautionary tale wrapped in throbbing guitars and atmospheric vocals.

'Diesel Breeze' (Johnson, Schermerhorn) 2:52

As with album opener 'Boiling Point', 'Diesel Breeze' was a hold-over from the aborted *Gun Sluts* sessions. Lyrically, it's rather sparse – an account of the desolation of the modern city: 'The train rises out of the dark/Above the boarded up boulevards/And burnt out cars'. There's an echo here of 1980s tracks like 'The Beat(en) Generation' and 'Heartland', but somehow more ground down, more hopeless. Johnson advises listeners to 'Conceal your fear/Pretend you've got no feelings to feel', the opposite message from 'Phantom Walls', which sees pain and fear as a motivating factor to instil change. Musically, this is a sample of the heavy, distorted sounds that Johnson and Schermerhorn had been cooking up in the *Gun Sluts* sessions, a short taster of what may have been a much longer jam. Stuck for lyrical inspiration, Johnson had turned to one of his past favourites, Wire's 'The Other Window' (chronicling a train journey in a foreign land), to provide the song's closing line, 'the other window has a better view', which otherwise may seem a non-sequitur.

'Weather Belle' 3:47

Perhaps the best song on the album, 'Weather Belle' has an uncanny resemblance to the Judy Garland torch song 'The Man That Got Away' as featured in the 1954 version of *A Star Is Born*. With music by Harold Arlen and lyrics by Ira Gershwin, it was nominated for a Best Original Song Oscar. Johnson must have been aware of it, but whether 'Weather Belle' is an unconscious imitation or a deliberate homage is unclear. There's a similarity to the rhythm and in the lyrics, even if Johnson's delivery gets nowhere near that of Garland. It's hard to ignore the similarity between the Arlen/Gershwin lines 'The night is bitter/The stars have lost their glitter/The winds grow colder/Suddenly you're older' and Johnson's 'And counting the laugh lines/On the face of the girl who stands in the doorway/And over her shoulder/There's a world growing colder/I'm feeling older and slowly less sober'. Johnson's song is about brief meetings and missed opportunities, the 'romance' of a one-night stand and the longing for more that can never be had: 'Nostalgia strikes hard at the heart/That cannot escape from its past'. As the chorus notes, the encounter describes a one-off, never-to-be-repeated event, but one that will live on in a yearning imagination: 'And it's the first and last time/That we'll ever meet/Strangers touching the parts/That love cannot reach'. The musicality lurches around in search of ever-elusive satisfaction. The track features Johnson playing an unusual instrument in the banjo, and a subject matter that he'd return to in the closing track of *Ensoulment*, 'A Rainy Day In May'.

'Voidy Numbness' (Johnson, Schermerhorn) 4:04

Fast-paced and aggressive, 'Voidy Numbness' (like album closer 'Salt Water') sees Johnson channelling the punk era he'd nearly missed. Loneliness and inability to strike up relationships is the subject matter, chronicling the failings of 21st-century men to escape the 'numbness' that contemporary culture instils: 'Can't love or be loved/Can't touch or be touched/Yes, he's lonely'. There's no escaping his unsatisfying life in another's arms: 'Another drink, another girl/Another life in another world/He's a phony'. The use of 'phony' to denote falseness recalls its earlier appearance on 'Boiling Point': 'Ever get lonely?/Don't you feel phony'. The closing line, 'Know his pain by its real name', is a prelude to 'Phantom Walls', about confronting pain to move past it.

'Phantom Walls' 4:17

Playing out like a lost cut from *Dusk*, 'Phantom Walls' came from Johnson's grief over his younger brother Eugene. It is lyrically accomplished and musically open, as the lyrics suggest that pain should be accepted rather than avoided as it motivates change: 'Pain can be your friend/As it explains/The answers to your questions/Consoles you in blue reflections/Listens to your soul's confessions/Then leads you in new directions'. Where 'Voidy Numbness' suggested that drinking ('He's drunk 25 pints of Amoco') is a way to suppress whatever's troubling, 'Phantom Walls' takes the opposite view – pain is to be welcomed as a motivation. It's a simple guitars-and-vocal two-hander between Johnson and Schermerhorn, and all the more effective for that. Johnson's whispery vocals and slow delivery seduce, building to the transcendent final verse: 'It's pain that stops the heart from

hating/That cures the mind of hesitating/That helps the soul in separating/
From everything that it's been blaming/Everything's changing'. Johnson's
falsetto returns for the ecstatic fade...

'Salt Water' (Johnson, Schermerhorn) 2:13
The nearest thing Johnson ever produced to punk, 'Salt Water' emerged from
the *Gun Sluts* sessions (as a co-write with Schermerhorn). It's a paean to
addiction, something Johnson knew a little about: 'Things get w-w-weird/
Before they go wrong/And he knows that once he starts/He just can't stop'.
It's an odd closer for an album that produced some striking and effective
ballads ('Shrunken Man', 'The Whisperers' and 'Weather Belle') that could
stand alongside anything from *Dusk*, some political and social point-scoring
('Global Eyes', 'Swine Fever') and a few bizarre experiments ('Boiling Point',
'Diesel Breeze', 'Voidy Numbness'). An artist should never stand still, but due
to the origins of *Naked Self* in the outré *Gun Sluts*, the final album seems
uneven.

Related Tracks
'Shrunken Man' 4:52
Four versions of *Naked Self*'s 'Shrunken Man' were released under the
Interpretations Issue 1 banner. Back in 2000, Johnson had conceived of
producing an album of cover versions of his work by others, perhaps inspired
by his takes on Hank Williams, but 'you can't release your own tribute album,
which is what it would look like. That idea started with 'Shrunken Man'.
Instead of getting people to remix it, I asked people to do different versions.'
The four-track 2000 Nothing Records CD included the original The The
version, followed by covers by experimental jazz group DAAU (4:50) from
Belgium, PJ Harvey collaborator John Parish (4:24) and Foetus (J. G.
Thirlwell) (5:01). The DAAU version goes big on strings (violin and cello),
initially recalling the Balanescu Quartet's takes on Kraftwerk on their 1992
album *Possessed*. The gentle strings and piano soon give way to harsh vocals
(in French) and dramatic drums. The take from Parish relies on gentle
acoustic guitar, flugelhorn from Mike Henning and languorous vocals from
Does De Wolf. Predictably, the Foetus version is the most abstract, with
threatening, ominous, very slow vocals against an atmospheric cacophony.
There was also a fifth take, titled 'Shrunken Man – Lunar Version' (3:10),
released on *Radio Cineola #14 Deep Space*.

'Gun Sluts' 3:53
The first release on Johnson's own Lazarus imprint was the title track from
the missing-in-action 1997 *Gun Sluts* abandoned album, released in 2000 in a
very limited edition sold on the *Naked Self* tour that year. An instrumental, it
features heavy reverb, distorted guitars and atmospheric sounds. The
dominant guitar riff is characteristic of The The, so it doesn't appear to be the

dramatic departure that Sony complained of. It does suggest that Johnson was prepared to take The The in a very different percussion-dominated direction before reverting to the safer sonic shores of *Naked Self*.

'Pillar Box Red' 4:00
Included on the 2002 *London Town* extra CD/DVD that accompanied the *London Town 1983-1993* box set, 'Pillar Box Red' was a promo single in 2002 for the *45RPM* singles compilation. A nostalgic piece, the song explores 'the country/Where I was born and bred' where 'Everything's changed/Though it seems the same'. Johnson returned to a changed (and changing) London and was determined to preserve his little corner of Shoreditch. He ultimately concludes, 'I love and hate this place/I ran away, but I couldn't escape'. The song has a lovely melodic structure, with Simon Hale on keyboards, Spencer Campbell on bass and Earl Harvin on drums. It anticipates *Ensoulment*, with this nostalgic songwriting further expressed in 'Mrs. Mac' and 'Down By The Frozen River'. Tim Pope shot the video in Bow's Palm Tree pub, featuring Johnson alongside family and friends.

'Deep Down Truth' 3:49
A new track included – alongside 'Pillar Box Red' – on the compilation *45RPM: The Singles Of The The*, 'Deep Down Truth' is one of the great overlooked The The songs. Charged with producing something with more potential 'popular' appeal than much of *Naked Self*, the song was recorded in the same session that produced 'Pillar Box Red' (under producers Clive Langer and Alan Winstanley) with the *Naked Self* band and backing vocals from Scottish-born Angela McCluskey (who performed in various American bands and worked with Cyndi Lauper). Johnson dug deep for his lyrics, adopting a big production sound. It's hugely optimistic, catchy and very singable – it's a shame it wasn't a single. There's something of the *James Bond* theme here, anticipating the even more Bond theme-like 'Darkness Cannot Exist In The Presence Of Light'. The song contrasts negative and positive emotions, suggesting one doesn't hold any more 'truth' than the other. The final verse turns things around, taking the song to a darker place: 'There's no more justice in peace than in war/There's no more time behind us than before'. It's one of Matt Johnson's most emotional, most commercial songs, and it was unfortunately buried as an 'extra' on a compilation album...

'In The AM' 24:49
Released as part of the 2002 *London Town* extra CD/DVD that accompanied the *London Town 1983-1993* box set, 'In The AM' was the most accomplished film music released by The The to that point. Assembled by Ian Peel, it was labelled an 'original soundtrack' from the film directed by Benn Northover. The film – unseen since 2002 – was part of the band's controversial 2002 Meltdown festival live performance at London's Southbank Centre (curated by

David Bowie). The performance featured just Johnson with J. G. Thirlwell working to pre-prepared tape loops and employing computer technology. It didn't go smoothly. The songs were stripped back, and the pair didn't entirely get to grips with the new technology. The chaotic performance split the crowd, some making their enthusiasm known while others walked out. The almost 25-minute 'In The AM' was part of the audio-visual presentation, playing out against images from Northover's film. Explaining the project, Johnson said it was 'not really music videos, more a combination of a short film with a music video.' Looking back from 2024 with Wesley Doyle, Johnson described the response to the event as 'really extreme, and in a way I kind of liked that rather than having a wishy-washy response. You had people absolutely loving it and others who, I was told, hated it so much that a fight broke out. It was radical and unusual, but my feeling is, if you like a record, it's not going anywhere, it's safe, trapped on vinyl or CD, and it's always going to sound the same. Why not be open-minded and allow [for] something different?' It was to be the last live performance by The The for 16 years. Also available at the event was the now exceedingly rare *Film Music* 2CD set (as was the 'Gun Sluts' CD single). The first CD, titled *Silent Tongue*, included many previously unreleased instrumental pieces plus some very early The The material. The second CD was the *45RPM* package.

'Mrs Mac' 2:32

Written around the same time as 'Pillar Box Red' and 'Deep Down Truth', the nostalgia-fest that is 'Mrs Mac' was released in various formats. In 2007, it was issued as a 'download single' as Johnson began to experiment with internet distribution. In 2023, it was also issued as the B-side to the single '$1 One Vote', giving the song a physical release. Johnson played all the instruments, and the song was produced by Bruce Lampcov. Johnson cited his first day at school as his inspiration: 'Mrs Mac was a sinister dinner lady/enforcer who terrorised the children into eating over-boiled slop that would make them heave in horror.' That's evident in lyrics like 'Mrs Mac, Mrs Mac/Answer back and you'll get more than a whack'! It could be the middle track in the nostalgia trilogy of 'Pillar Box Red', 'Mrs Mac' and – much later – 'Down By The Frozen River' on *Ensoulment*.

The The Miscellany

Why did Matt Johnson disappear for the better part of 25 years? The answer is that he didn't, not entirely. He may not have been making music, but he was occupied in other ways. The lack of promotion behind *Naked Self* and the requirement to self-fund much of the subsequent tour took its toll on Johnson's physical and mental health. It's little wonder that after such a massive setback, he would take time for himself, retreat from music and performance and concentrate on his family life.

All the while, Johnson continued to write songs. A holiday break in the autumn of 2000 at the home of a friend in Woodstock saw Johnson working with a portable studio set-up and composing new songs, including the nostalgic pairing of 'Mrs Mac' and 'Pillar Box Red', and one of The The's best tracks, the hugely optimistic 'Deep Down Truth'. There wasn't a lack of creativity, just a lack of liquidity. By the summer of 2001, Johnson and St Michaels relocated to her native Sweden, renting out their properties in New York and London. Shortly after, Johnson's mother died. By 2003, he'd sold the New York property and bought a place in Sweden. Johnson never settled into life in Sweden, and when St Michael's photography career took off, he felt their relationship was drawing to a close.

The only music released during this period was the 2002 remastered editions of *Soul Mining, Infected, Mind Bomb* and *Dusk* (collected in the *London Town 1983-1993* box set), and the *45RPM: The Singles Of The The*, which collected the main singles and some oddities, including the original takes of 'Uncertain Smile' and 'Perfect', the *Disinfected* version of 'This Is The Day', a reworked 'December Sunlight' (from *Naked Self*) and the two new tracks, 'Pillar Box Red' and 'Deep Down Truth'. A disc of 12" remixes accompanied the singles collection. These releases helped keep The The afloat in the first decade of the 21st century.

For the three years following the end of his relationship, Johnson lived a nomadic lifestyle, flitting between London, Sweden, Spain and New York. 'I was like a man on the run,' Johnson told biographer Neil Fraser, 'trying to escape from my own life...' In the two decades since 1993's *Dusk*, the music industry had changed, and Johnson couldn't see where he fitted in. Having signed 'bad' deals with Cherry Red and with CBS, he was wary of becoming beholden to a record company where management and ownership could change in the blink of an eye. In the growing internet, Johnson perceived a model of production that might offer him control over the creation and distribution of new music through new technology, but it would be a slow process getting there.

His interest in music having diminished, Johnson found new things to fill his time: photography, writing, travelling and continuing his autodidactic mission through reading recent volumes on global politics. The world was changing, but Johnson wondered if he had the strength to change with it. Along with the growing self-doubt, he found himself turning to alcohol, partly as an antidote to his grief and to being separated from his son, Jackson. For the majority of the first decade of the 21st century, Johnson didn't so much pick up a guitar or write any new material.

Recognising his friend in the text of John Tottenham's 2004 book of poems *The Inertia Variations*, J. G. Thirlwell sent a copy to Johnson. The songwriter read the book in one sitting, coming to the conclusion: 'This is me!' Having captured Johnson's own inability to get down to productive work, Tottenham's book spurred the reluctant musician into action. He contacted the author, hoping to create some new work based on the book. The match between the subject matter and the state Johnson found himself in was exact, but being stuck in such a creative limbo also didn't bode well for actually producing anything. Although nothing came of it in the short term, the idea would not leave Johnson, even while he avoided doing any work on it at all...

Johnson had other things going on, including a new relationship. He'd met Helen Edwards at a party, and a relationship developed. At the same time, Johnson reclaimed his Shoreditch property, and in 2008, built a £125,000 home recording studio (paid for by allowing his music to be used in TV adverts, notably in a US campaign promoting M&Ms). A return to music-making seemed inevitable, but it still didn't happen.

Instead, in 2010, Johnson inaugurated a series of 15-minute internet broadcasts/podcasts under the *Radio Cineola* banner. Intended to mimic the shortwave radio broadcasts from Radio Caroline and Radio Luxembourg he'd listened to in his bedroom in his youth, the format allowed Johnson to explore a variety of interests, interviewing people whose ideas he found fascinating, presenting previously unheard material from his archives and providing a showcase for his collaborators. He also embarked upon composing music for movies. Although he'd already created soundtracks for St Michael's shorts, it was the debut of his brother Gerard as the director of 2009's comic serial killer movie *Tony* that saw Johnson morph into a fully-fledged soundtrack composer, adopting a sparse piano-driven approach. The first *Radio Cineola* included cuts from *Tony*, samples from the Johnson-focused documentary *The Inertia Variations* (2017) and a 'new' track, 'Slow Rider', pulled from Johnson's unreleased material. This would set the pattern for the following 18 instalments, released on a roughly monthly basis.

With the launch of *Radio Cineola*, things began to flow. Johnson didn't feel the pressure of a 'pop' career, with no record label demanding new material and no audience with any expectation that he'd produce anything anytime soon. He was free to do what he liked, indulge himself at his own pace. He scored a second soundtrack job when he composed the music for Nichola Bruce's 2010 documentary *Moonbug*, about the 1969 Moon landing Apollo pioneers (the soundtrack was released by Johnson as Volume 2 in the independently released *Cineola* soundtrack series).

At the same time, Johnson became heavily involved in local politics and campaigns focused on preserving the historic East End of London. That kept him occupied, as did the birth of a second son, named George, in April 2012, with his partner Helen. Life was ticking over nicely when tragedy struck – Matt's brother Andrew, the man behind so many of the images on The The record sleeves across the years, was diagnosed with an aggressive brain tumour. Given six months to live, Andrew would defy that outlook, living for a further four years. Johnson's activities with the East End Preservation Society served as a distraction from the reality of Andrew's predicament. Johnson would eventually withdraw from these activities to instead focus on restoring his own building.

In 2014, with the 30th anniversary of *Soul Mining*, Johnson emerged into the public spotlight once more (albeit rather reluctantly) to celebrate. As part of that, Kevin Foakes, billed as 'DJ Food', released a 12" vinyl remix of 'GIANT' for Record Store Day – releases for this celebration of recorded music and record stores would feature heavily for Johnson over the next few years as a way of testing the waters for new musical material. Inevitably, at the Q&A session at Rough Trade for *Soul Mining*, Johnson was asked about new music. Johnson told *The Quietus*: 'I do get a tingling when I think about it ... especially with all the geopolitical stuff going on...'

The next release from Johnson was more soundtrack music for Gerard Johnson's 2014 neo-noir crime thriller *Hyena*. Johnson also appeared in a film – The The fan J. J. Abrams, then making the 'comeback' *Star Wars* movie *The Force Awakens* (2015) at Pinewood, invited Johnson to play a background character. The exploration of his own archive through the *Radio Cineola* broadcasts and his soundtrack work had slowly but surely created a desire in Johnson for a full return to creating music. Unfortunately, his timing was off: his long-awaited return to touring in 2018 was followed by the debilitating COVID-19 pandemic that put the entire world into a form of inertia. Not for nothing did the lyrics of 'Soul Mining' include the lines: 'Something always goes wrong/When things are going right...'

Soundtracks By The The/Matt Johnson

Gerard Johnson's first movie was shot around London on an extremely tight budget of just £40,000. *Tony* (2009) starred his cousin Peter Ferdinando as the hapless, socially anxious, Dennis Nilsen-like serial killer. Gory – yet very funny – Johnson's movie (expanded from an earlier short) won the New Visions award at the Sitges International Film Festival in 2010. Luckily, when it came to scoring, Johnson had a brother who knew a little something about music. Matt Johnson's self-produced score was based around a strong piano line (with opening track 'The Lust For Unsung Dreams' setting the tone), with Johnson playing all the instruments including the melodica, a Moog synth, an acoustic bass guitar and a return to the tape loops he'd used as a teenager. Gerard wrote in the liner notes: 'I always found Matt's music cinematic ... [He] created a delicate yet haunting soundscape, [with] a melodic, [yet] sparse structure that enhances the film's atmosphere.' The result is unmistakably a work by The The capturing the ominous nature of the city.

Johnson followed that up with Nichola Bruce's documentary *Moonbug* (2010), which followed photographer Steve Pyke as he travelled to meet his childhood heroes, America's lunar astronauts. Once more, the score was a one-man band, with Johnson utilising tape loops, piano, synths, guitars and percussion to achieve an other-worldly sound.

Then, it was back to working with Gerard again on the scores for crime drama *Hyena* (2014) and the bodybuilding psychodrama *Muscle* (2019). On *Hyena*, Johnson employs some familiar The The sounds (especially from *Dusk*) to capture a threatening version of London's underworld. The Mellotron and the Omnichord were dug out for the black-and-white *Muscle*, which also included a song by The The, 'I Want 2 B U'. Johnson has at least three or four further movie scores in the works, including that for Gerard Johnson's next film, *Odyssey* (2025).

Radio Cineola Podcasts

'Slow Rider' 4:28 (*Radio Cineola 1: Arrival*)

While the first *Radio Cineola* podcast in March 2010 focused on Johnson's score for the movie *Tony* (2009), featuring the track 'The Lust For Unsung Dreams' and a couple of excerpts from *The Inertia Variations*, it also included this track 'from the vaults'. It was previously released on the rare *Film Music* CD. It's a mood piece, with an opening reminiscent of Gabriel Yared's score for the 1986 movie *Betty Blue*. Unexpectedly, the vocals then cut in: 'Where do all the days go...?' It's unclear when it was recorded, but it is certainly pre-2002, though it doesn't feel like a cut from *Naked Self*. Johnson comes to an unusual conclusion with the line 'Life is sweeter than mystery', something he might not agree with today when *Ensoulment*'s 'Life After Life' features the lines 'The strange becomes familiar, the familiar strange/Some things best experienced, not explained...'

'Darkness Cannot Exist In The Presence Of Light' 3:26 (*Radio Cineola 3: The Presence Of Light*)

While the second *Radio Cineola* podcast (*51st State Cafe*) didn't feature any new music, the third entry hit it out of the park with the inclusion of 'Darkness Cannot Exist In The Presence Of Light', billed as being by 'The The & Deadly Avenger'. It's a big, brassy number, The The's version of a glorious Bond theme – it's a shame that very few people heard it. The big sound here might be no surprise as 'Deadly Avenger' is film composer and dance music artist Damon Baxter, billed as a pioneer of the 'big beat' sound. Big on strings, crossed with gritty beats, Baxter scored multiple car ads, then movie trailers.

The combination of Baxter's 'big' sound with Johnson's impactful vocals and lyrics helped create one of The The's best (and least heard) tracks. Johnson's lyrics pre-echo some of his concerns explored more fully on *Ensoulment*: 'To learn to live, you had to die/That a death of the body, but a death of the pride/That separates the soul from mind'. Of course, time and its passing is another well-worn The The concern: 'It's too late to hesitate/ Time will have its say.'

'The Answer To When Is Now' 2:52 (*RC3*)
Billed as a 'work in progress', 'The Answer...' is a pulsing slice of electronica that isn't very The The-like until the keyboards hit, but which plays out like a soundtrack for an imaginary film...

'No Hiding Place' 3.36 (*RC3*)
From the legendary unreleased *Spirits* album, 'No Hiding Place' appeared in 2010 as part of the third *Radio Cineola* podcast. Musically, 'No Hiding Place' was a first draft of 'Slow Train To Dawn' from 1986's *Infected*. More guitar-heavy and featuring different lyrics/vocals, it was another pointer to the sound that Johnson was working towards, one different from his early works.

'Me And My Shadow' 1:09 (*Radio Cineola 4: April Fools*)
Following early The The member Colin Lloyd Tucker's Bowie-inspired take on 'Perfect', there's a brief rendering of this traditional song, with Johnson on vocals and Tucker on the 'old Joanna' (piano) – a pub singalong of the sort Johnson grew up with. A curiosity, followed by a brief, Arabic-sounding, atmospheric instrumental 'Sign Of Good Faith' (a Tucker and Johnson co-write).

'The 51st State' 3:02 (*RC4*)
Riffing on the climactic lines from 'Heartland', the under-three-minute live performance of 'The 51st State' that concludes the fourth *Radio Cineola* podcast is a slow, melodic repackage of the original.

'Something Strange' 1:18 (*Radio Cineola 5: Mayday Mayday*)
Playing out against various found sounds of foreign radio broadcasts, 'Something Strange' (billed as 'from the vaults') sounds like a *Burning Blue Soul* era experiment in layered sonic ambience. A guitar riff reinforces that, with the young Johnson playing with tape loops. The production gets progressively less 'muddy' as it goes on, perhaps an abandoned tune that Johnson failed to finish.

'God's Audience' 6:26 (*RC5*)
Billed as from 'somewhere far out into space', 'God's Audience' is a breezy atmosphere piece from *Electronium*, also the name of an early electronic synthesiser. A distorted, slowed voice reads a sci-fi story that riffs on Stanley Kubrick's *2001: A Space Odyssey*. Synth drones and sweeping tones conclude this proto-film music, sounding like a lost cut from *Blade Runner*.

'Mood Elevator' 1:15 (RC5)

A one-minute riff on familiar The The themes, perhaps discarded from an uncompleted track.

'Justice 4 Jesus' 3:06 (*Radio Cineola 6: Blue Moon In June*)

Radio Cineola 6 opens with a chat with *Hanky Panky* and *Naked Self* era guitarist Eric Schermerhorn – Johnson says they have worked together on four albums, but only two have been released. The two unreleased albums named were *Gun Sluts* and the previously unknown *2 Blocks Below Canal* (which, with *Naked Self*, would have formed a New York Trilogy). 'Justice 4 Jesus', which later morphed into '$1 One Vote', is said to have come from *2 Blocks Below Canal*, although the accompanying text on the website states it is a 'rough mix from *Karmic Gravity*', another The The mystery.

This early version of '$1 One Vote' has almost all the elements in place, though it starts off a little more laid back and lacks the concluding line that Johnson finally found.

'Psychic Sauna' 4:40 (RC6)

A previously unreleased cut ('rough mix') from *Gun Sluts*, 'Psychic Sauna' features a strummed guitar over which reversed electronic bleeps play out as a melody slowly builds against babble from short wave broadcasts. It sounds more like a freewheeling jam than the supposedly hard-to-take 'experimental' noises that *Gun Sluts* threatened.

Music From Je T'aime Infiniment (2012) (*Radio Cineola 7: En Route To Beirut*)

Featuring five tracks from *Je T'aime Infiniment* (*I Love You So Much*), a 2012 Danish, 21-minute short made entirely in Lebanon, written and directed by Nikolaj Bendix Skyum Larsen and Corine Shawi (who introduces this podcast), about the secrets kept by two elderly sisters. Johnson scored the film, with the soundtrack taking up the bulk of *Radio Cineola 7*. 'Silent Together' is a slow-moving piano doodle, followed by 'Splayed!', a more discordant, but equally slow-paced piano riff mixed with soundtrack effects. 'Tender Mercy' lightens things a little, and sounds more like a The The track, building a tune from simple keyboard work.

For 'The Rain Inside', similar motifs continue the theme, while 'Does Prayer Work?' concludes the music from *Je T'aime Infiniment* in atmospheric style. It's a minor work, but at least it's available for those who want to seek it out.

'Lip Tripping' 2:33 (RC7)

'Lip Tripping' concluded *Radio Cineola 7* in queasy style. It's an instrumental, harmonica-driven track with an *Infected* era feel, perhaps an off-cut from those sessions. It could easily have served as a B-side at the time.

'Life Of Lies' 2:30 (*Radio Cineola 8: In The City Of The Angels*)
The first of two tracks from the 2010 short documentary *Bilder Av Dina* (*About Dina*) about a former model plagued by rumours of criminal activity. The film was made by Johnson's former partner Johanna St Michaels, who was once a client of the titular Dina Ziegler Panagiotou when she was an agent. 'Life Of Lies' is more rhythmic than anything from *Je T'aime Infiniment*, but still largely piano-based, with enough echoes of former The The work to make it of interest.

'The Arrest' 3:28 (*RC8*)
The second of two tracks from that 2010 short, 'The Arrest' initially suggests a sense of a world spinning out of control, a slightly queasy take on the Hollywood dream. It then becomes a dynamic, piano-driven track, augmented with strings, suggesting a thriller or crime movie.

'Spirals' 0:47 (*RC8*)
Billed as from *Electronium*, 'Spirals' is made up of woozy synth lines that wax and wane for just under a minute. It's followed by 'Big Bad Boomby', credited to 'Matthew & Son', Johnson and his younger son George (who also introduced this edition of *Radio Cineola*), who says 'This song was named after me' and also seems to feature George on vocals – something of a parental indulgence.

Various Instrumentals 15:00 (*Radio Cineola 9: Fear & Loathing In The Las Vegas Of The North*)
Released with no information as to their source, eight tracks made up *Radio Cineola 9*. The eight tracks are 'Sentimental Journey', 'Dark City', 'Placebo Trip', 'Tune Into My Waves', 'Kebabylon', 'Rollin' Across My Mind', 'My Old Mate' and 'Night Duty', interspersed with dialogue possibly lifted from a documentary. Yet another The The mystery... It plays out with an apparent on-site street recording of 'I Do Like To Be Beside The Seaside'.

Moonbug Soundtrack (*Radio Cineola 10: Fly Me To The Moon*)
Radio Cineola 10 features no new musical material.

'Body Bonfire' 2:30 (*Radio Cineola 11: Remember, Remember*)
Following the *Judge Dredd* movie soundtrack cut 'Darkness Falls', *Radio Cineola 11* unveils a trio of tracks billed as being from *Electronium*: 'First Light', 'Drowler' and 'Avail', all atmospheric synth drones. The most interesting, previously unreleased cut, though, is 'Body Bonfire', a 'rough mix' of a rejected track from *Naked Self*. It's clearly an instrumental first take on ideas that would become the musical bed for 'Swine Fever'.

'Winter Light' 1:27 (*Radio Cineola 12: Blow, Blow Thou Winter Wind*)
The 12th *Radio Cineola* package included the first release of the demo of the cracking 'Deep Down Truth' with Angela McCluskey, plus another jangly track

from *Electronium* titled 'Shiver' (2:36). More worthwhile is the unattributed 'Winter Light', a twinkly atmospheric piece with wind effects.

'A Reflection On 9/11' (*Radio Cineola 13: Ten Years After*)
This is a spoken-word essay seemingly written by Johnson on 9/11 conspiracies, but narrated by a synthetic-sounding or treated voice billed as 'Arthur Dinklebottom'. The following *Radio Cineola* editions 14-18 are spoken word and interview instalments lacking new or previously unheard music, while editions 19-30 are dedicated to the *Midday To Midnight* 2015 live UK general election internet broadcast curated by Johnson and edited into roughly one-hour slices. All are available on the The The website.

Official Bootlegs
Official Bootleg Volume 001
'Love Lamp' 6:04
Following the *Gun Sluts* draft of 'Boiling Point' (revised and released on *Naked Self*), The The's *Official Bootleg Volume 001* offers up the first of five newly released tracks from *Gun Sluts*. 'Love Lamp' is a rough sonic mix of feedback and harsh noise, with some lyrical distorted guitar poking through. It's a hazy, hallucinogenic sound, like industrial psychedelia. Not easy listening, but kinda interesting – you can see why the suits at Sony threw up their hands in despair...

'Fuck Wit' 2:59
This one appeared on *Naked Self* in slightly revised form as 'Diesel Breeze', with a vignette of New York nighttime city life added in brief but descriptive lyrics by Johnson.

'Kid Killers' 3:38
The harsh *Gun Sluts* sounds continue with gung-ho guitars reprising some of the sounds from 'Boiling Point' before drowning in feedback. It sounds like all involved had fun playing these industrial jams, until the label asked for a sellable album...

'Echo Plasm' 2:03
Two minutes of hums and drones.

'60 BPM' 8:12
An eight-minute epic, containing musical themes from bits of *Naked Self* and yet more of the *Gun Sluts* self-indulgence. It's a worthwhile track with just enough of the unique The The DNA buried in the mix to make it worth listening to.

Official Bootleg Volumes 002-009
002: A live recording of an unnamed gig from the 1990 *The The Versus The World* tour.

003: Nine tracks from Johnson's early days as part of The Gadgets, featuring the two most notable songs from this period, the mesmerising melodic 'There Over There' (4:43) and 'Devil's Dyke' (3:08) – both could easily pass as early The The songs. The other tracks are more musical doodles, either instrumentals or vocally-light: 'Six Mile Bottom' (2:19), 'Sliddery' (1:43), 'She's Queen Of Toyland' (1:47), 'Slepe' (0:46), 'Autumn '80 (Cripes)' (2:15) and the more substantial, brooding 'Checking To Make Sure' (3:26) and the wittily-titled 'Duplicate (Original Version)' (3:35), sounding like a Radiophonic Workshop *Doctor Who* score of the 1980s. Also included were two new, but relatively inessential live performances by Colin Lloyd Tucker and Matt Johnson: a cover of The Velvet Underground's 'What Goes On' (4:05) and 'The Azimuth Key' (2:39).
004: A live recording of an unnamed gig from the 1993 European leg of the *Lonely Planet* tour.
005: An acoustic set performed live on the radio during the American leg of the *Naked Self* tour.
006: Recorded in Holland in early 1995 during The The's rehearsals for a pan-European tour.
007: A live recording from the end of the *Naked Self* tour in Cologne, Germany, December 2000.
008: A live recording from a US date from the 1989 *The The Versus The World* tour.
009: Expanded demo versions of tracks previously excerpted on the *Radio Cineola* podcasts, including 'Slow Rider' (4:53), 'Deep Down Truth' (3:47), 'Pillar Box Red' (3:52), 'The 51st State' (3:02), 'Armageddon Days (mezcal mix)' (2:59), 'Global Eyes (drumless version)' (3:26), 'Shrunken Man (lunar version)' (3:07), 'Drowler' (1:45), 'Hidden' (1:34, a previously unreleased short, pulsing, rhythmic blast), 'Me And My Shadow' (1:04) and 'Flesh & Bones (Meltdown rehearsal)' – a rather languorous take.

Cineola Miscellany

A selection of some of Johnson's favourite self-composed film music from *Tony*, *Moonbug* and *Hyena*, including a trio of previously unreleased tracks. The atmospheric 'The Late Station' (2:13), billed as 'from the forthcoming soundtrack album *Midnight To Midnight*; melodic 'Sunset In The City' (1:51), billed as being 'from the forthcoming soundtrack album *Oden*'; and the chunky 'The Changing Colours Of The Sky' (3:06), billed as 'from the forthcoming soundtrack album *Helios*'. All three are works-in-progress from future, as yet unreleased, films.

Ensoulment (2024)

Personnel:
Matt Johnson: vocals, acoustic guitar, electric guitar, drum machine, tambourine
Barrie Cadogan: backing vocals, electric guitar
James Eller: bass guitar
Earl Harvin: drums
DC Collard: keyboards
Terry Edwards: horns
Danny Cummings: percussion
Sonya Cullingford: vielle, fiddle, strings
Gillian Glover: backing vocals
Recorded at Real World Studios, Corsham; Studio Cineola, London, between 2023 and 2024
Producers: Matt Johnson, Warne Livesey
Label: Cineola/Ear Music
Release date: 6 September 2024 (UK)
Charts: UK: 19, Aus: 15, Ger: 11, Netherlands: 79, Switzerland: 54
Running time: 45:38
All tracks written by Matt Johnson, except where stated

The Inertia Variations documentary project, ironically, would serve to break Matt Johnson out of the state of ennui and creative inactivity that had plagued him for over a decade. He missed songwriting, if not the business that surrounded making music or the need to perform live. His *Radio Cineola* project had served to re-interest him in his own back catalogue and had confirmed that he still had an audience, something he feared he'd lost. He felt the time was right to make a return to music.

Something that helped was his hiring of Gillian Glover. She was a musician in her own right (and the daughter of a musician father) who'd worked at Dessau in New York in the 1990s when Johnson had been recording there. She was charged with creating a professional infrastructure for Johnson to realise his slowly developing new ambition to be in control of his own output. That meant running the recording studio, managing the Johnson-owned record label, arranging the manufacturing of CDs and vinyl and supervising the press and PR operation to get the news of Johnson's formal return to music-making out to his fans. Without that structure in place, it is doubtful he would have had the confidence to make the effort to revive his musical career.

Finally, the time was also right to return to *The Inertia Variations*, the long-form poem that had haunted Johnson. It was his ex-partner, Johanna St Michaels, who suggested turning her filmmaker's eye on Johnson himself. Over time, the project grew into a multi-media experience, fulfilling one of the oft-neglected aims that Johnson had when establishing The The as an arts collective back in the 1980s. Speaking to *First Avenue,* Johnson commented on *The Inertia Variations*: 'It was a fruition of those early ideas of The The, to be genuinely mixed media, to go off in various tangents and do something that's very, very unusual.' He expanded on what he'd achieved for the *Brooklyn Vegan*: 'Diving into that project about inertia actually cured my procrastination, and it became a very intense project. There was a radio show (*Radio Cineola*), we had a couple of art exhibitions. There was a book, a film and, out of that, [a] new song, 'We Can't Stop What's Coming'.'

Filming on the documentary, like many of Johnson's projects, took time. Looking for a 'hook', St Michaels pitched a live 12-hour *Radio Cineola* podcast covering the May 2015 General Election and featuring many of Johnson's past collaborators, as well as various commentators. That was combined with Johnson's focus on renovating his Shoreditch building and the creation of a nine-metre-high radio tower. That was then further combined with another day's filming in May 2016, capturing the process of other artists covering Johnson's songs. The final part of the package was Johnson's narration of the Tottenham poem that had inspired the entire project.

The package was released as the *Radio Cineola Trilogy* in 2017. Following the first three soundtrack releases (*Tony, Moonbug* and *Hyena*), *Cineola Volume 4: The End Of The Day* was a disc of covers and the new song 'We Can't Stop What's Coming'. *Cineola Volume 5: The Inertia Variations* was Johnson's reading of an edited version of the poem, while *Cineola Volume 6: Midday To Midnight* was extracted from the live 2015 election broadcast. The book that Johnson referenced was 2012's *Tales From The Two Puddings*, a memoir by Johnson's publican father Eddie, published by his own imprint, 51st State Press. The exhibition accompanied the screening of *The Inertia Variations* documentary at the Edinburgh Film Festival.

For someone struck by inertia, Johnson had hit a very busy period, although only one new song emerged. The death of Andrew Johnson in January 2016 had helped fuel Johnson's new activity, both as a way of coping with his personal grief and as a way of honouring his brother. As well as the song 'We Can't Stop What's Coming', Johnson continued to use his brother's art on many of his new projects, including on the cover of the 2024 album *Ensoulment*. The long-awaited return to live performance in 2018 and the issuing of *The Comeback Special* on CD, vinyl and DVD were also part of the effort by Johnson to honour Andrew and the death of Johnson's father, Eddie, in 2018, aged 86, just as *The Comeback Special* tour was kicking off. 'I've tried to use [grief] as a form of therapy', Johnson told *The Irish Times*. 'Using it as a way of expressing very deep feelings. It's the only way I can respond to those situations … turn[ing] it into something positive.'

The announcement that The The would return to playing live – for the first time in 16 years – had been long awaited. A fan base, long starved of new music and live performances, quickly ensured that the first dates, at the Royal Albert Hall and the Brixton Academy, sold out in minutes. What would become known as the 2018 *Comeback Special* (knowingly referring to the

1968 Elvis Presley TV show the *68 Comeback Special*) grew in size due to demand, with dates added across the UK, the US, Canada and festival gigs at the Heartland Festival in Denmark (named after Johnson's 1986 song) and at Festival No. 6 at Portmerion in Wales. Johnson feared there would be little interest in him and his music after such a long period. The rapturous welcome to the tour gave him new confidence and set him on the road that would lead to the first new The The album in almost 25 years. In the *Official Tour Book*, Johnson noted: 'As I hadn't performed live in years, people asked if I had concerns that there would be enough interest for a The The tour. I had a pretty humble attitude ... I was, however, pleasantly surprised and happy that so many concerts sold out so quickly.'

In putting together the band for the tour, Johnson made the inspired decision to involve members from all three previous tours. 'It's nice to have one member from each of those bands,' he told Neil Fraser, 'and then a new member for this one.' The lineup included James Eller, from the *The The Versus The World* tour; Collard on keyboards, from the *Lonely Planet* tour; Harvin on drums, from the *Naked Self* tour (due to other commitments, Harvin was replaced by Geoff Dugmore for the Australian leg); and 'new boy' Barrie Cadogan, who'd been recommended to Johnson by Johnny Marr. Cadogan had written the theme tune to the US TV series *Better Call Saul*, a show Johnson had enjoyed. Preparations for the tour and intense rehearsals began in March 2018. Their rationale was not to reproduce the songs from the earlier albums (Johnson suggested anyone wanting to hear those arrangements should put on the album), but to adapt them to the five-member band.

After the tour and just as Johnson discovered new momentum, everything worldwide came to a halt due to the COVID-19 pandemic, with 'lockdowns' confining many to their homes throughout much of 2020 and into 2021. Johnson reverted to old habits, taking advantage of the empty streets and silence to walk his neighbourhood (and far beyond). He also found himself engaging with the politics of the response to the virus, considering the power that authorities had to direct and control individuals. Johnson began exploring – via the internet – what some might tag as 'conspiracy theories'. This material would eventually inform some of his new songs.

Then, illness struck. Beginning as a sore throat in the spring of 2020, Johnson developed a 'throbbing' pain on one side of his neck. As the problem grew, he found himself in the Royal Free Hospital at Whitechapel, an event he recalled as an 'eerie' experience, as the wards were closed due to the pandemic. Scans and tests revealed a pharyngeal abscess, which required an operation. This put the fear into Johnson: as a singer, he relied on his voice, something he'd only just recovered after a long time away. Would he still be able to sing? Would he sound the same? The operation was successful, but as Johnson explained: 'Doctor's orders mean I cannot sing for the next six months, and even when I can, I'm not sure if I'll sound like Howlin' Wolf or

Tiny Tim! Hopefully I'll still sound like myself.' A long, slow recovery followed, and his voice finally returned in fine fettle.

Lockdown afforded Johnson the time to tackle something he'd long put off: exploring his own musical archives. Digging through taped material spanning four decades, much of it unlabelled, Johnson recovered and remastered a variety of his past output, releasing them as the *Official Bootleg* CD series [see previous chapter]. Material from long-abandoned projects, such as tracks from *Gun Sluts*, *Spirits* and others, finally saw the light of day as official, remastered releases.

As the world emerged from lockdown, Johnson's thoughts turned to getting the band back together – literally. Partly, the time and space he'd had in lockdown had focused his mind on songwriting, and the politics of the pandemic had provided new targets for his ire. Talking to *Flood* magazine, Johnson admitted: 'It just got to the point where I felt very driven. Particularly, the state of the world: we're living through very interesting times. A lot of big changes. There's a lot of disorientation. It's quite a fertile time, creatively, I think.' Although Johnson had closed The Garden studio in 2012 as a commercial concern, he still owned it, so he had a ready-made recording facility and a ready-made band. The obvious thing was to reconvene the 2018 *Comeback Special* band.

As well as Eller from the *Mind Bomb* period, Johnson called on producer Warne Livesey to preside over the new work. 'We'd kept in touch and I felt this was the right project to bring him back', Johnson told the *Brooklyn Vegan*:

> We had a great time, the wonderful band, the musicians are terrific ... A lot of the album was recorded live. We went to Peter Gabriel's place in Somerset, Real World Studios ... We had rehearsed for a week at my place, and we went down there for a week, and because they're such good musicians, I wanted to record it fairly live. Then, we brought it back to my studio to do the overdubs. I'm really pleased with the way it turned out. I think it fits very well alongside the other albums, which is really important to me.

Johnson was only too aware that his return to creative work came in the wake of the death of his brother Andrew, just as 'Love Is Stronger Than Death' had been written in tribute to Eugene. It was 'We Can't Stop What's Coming', the song written in response to Andrew's diagnosis, that unblocked Johnson. 'It was during his illness and his passing away that inspired me to write that song, and that kick-started my creativity', he said. 'It was ironic, really, that my inertia slowly crept in after my younger brother Eugene died. I found it harder and harder to create. It's somehow strange that it took the passing of another brother to then bring me back to full creativity.'

Ensoulment hit number 19 on the UK Album Chart in its first week of release – not bad after a near 25-year gap between albums (it reached number six on the mid-week update chart and number two on the Scottish

Album Chart). Johnson's return as The The with *Ensoulment* was largely welcomed by critics. Perhaps his 'elder statesman' status, at the age of 62, differentiated him enough from the 'angry young man' phase that saw him through the 1980s and 1990s?

Writing in *The Scotsman*, Fiona Shepherd welcomed the return of 'the brooding ambience and quiet rage' that was Johnson's trademark. *Far Out* magazine complained about the 'wordiness' of this 'perplexing new album'. Writer Dale Maplethorpe noted the breadth of subject matter across the 12 tracks: 'Everything happening today, from the big picture of artificial intelligence to the small issue of a breaking heart, no stone is left unturned.' Despite that mild criticism, the album was 'a real treat to listen to'. *Spill* magazine noted that 'Johnson's storytelling and voice continue to be as captivating and compelling as ever', while *The Line Of Best Fit* said: '*Ensoulment* doesn't shy away from confronting raw emotions, but nevertheless finds time for wry humour in amongst the essential soul-searching.' For *MOJO*, 'these 12 songs cement Johnson's 'cherishable agitator' status. And – whisper it – there's hope here, too.' According to Wesley Doyle in *Record Collector*, *Ensoulment* displayed 'a comforting, analogue hum', helping to create 'the warm, dusty sound instantly recognisable as The The'. He concluded: 'As an artist known for rallying against the injustices of the world, Johnson could have created an album of unremitting gloom given the current state of global affairs. It's to his credit that *Ensoulment* is a welcome – and hopeful – return from a man who obviously still has much to offer.'

Matt Johnson had choreographed an amazing comeback after a long time away, but he still felt he had more to offer. 'I wish I'd made more albums, in some ways', he admitted to *Flood* magazine. 'All the albums I've made, I'm proud of. They're all albums that were made for the right reasons, and I tried as hard as I could. There's no record I've put out that I've regretted. God willing, there'll be a few more albums to come!' The 'comeback' that The The kicked off in 2017 had finally reached fruition with 2024's *Ensoulment*.

'Cognitive Dissident' (Matt Johnson, Barrie Cadogan) 3:06
Perhaps a surprising choice for an opener, 'Cognitive Dissident' clearly builds on tracks like '$1 One Vote' in its lyrical obsessions. As the prelude to the first album from The The in almost a quarter of a century (it reached a peak of number four on the UK Vinyl Singles Chart), the song continues Johnson's focus on the changing meaning of language, where new uses seem predicated on Orwellian visions. 'We certainly live in interesting times', said Johnson of this first single. 'The world is becoming more inverted, weird and hallucinogenic by the day.' Opening with a blast of dissonance, the sounds quickly clarify as percussion and guitar take over. A sequel to *Naked Self*'s 'Global Eyes', Johnson adopts the same contrasted word play: 'Left is right, black is white/Inside out, hope is doubt/Below above, hate is love/Upside down, square is round/War is peace, West is East'. Johnson engages directly

with the wave of disinformation sweeping society, often from those in positions of power, with 'Truth lies on the gallows/Lies sit on the throne'. Johnson told *The Irish Times*:

> It's a general metaphor about power. The truth is now so ridiculed, disbelieved and marginalised. We live in a society where the politicians lie, the media lie – about everything, all the time. That's why the trust in politicians and trust in the mainstream media is on the floor. People aren't stupid. Their instinct tells them, 'This person is lying to me'. Lies have become the currency of the day.

It would be a rich vein that Johnson would further explore in other 'political' tracks on this album, including 'Kissing The Ring Of POTUS' and 'Linoleum Smooth To The Stockinged Foot'. One thing the track lacks is a definitive ending – it doesn't build to a climax (as '$1 One Vote' did) and instead simply fades away. The B-side was the previously unreleased 'When Is The Heart Of Waiting' (4:15), an instrumental driven by distorted guitars and pulsing synths to melancholic effect. The title suggests this may have been a very early version of *Naked Self*'s 'Phantom Walls'.

'Some Days I Drink My Coffee By The Grave Of William Blake' 4:03
Another 'state of the nation' song, this one is not as angry as 'Heartland' or 'The Beat(en) Generation'. It's more a lament for a lost Britain (or, more specifically, a lost England) that has changed beyond all recognition from Johnson's childhood in the 1960s and his young adulthood in the 1980s. It's another London song, in the tradition of tracks like 'Perfect', 'Flesh And Bones', 'Helpline Operator' and 'Pillar Box Red'. It was released as the third single from *Ensoulment*, following 'Cognitive Dissident' and 'Linoleum Smooth To The Stockinged Foot', and it reached the top spot on the UK Vinyl Singles Chart – quite an achievement. The B-side instrumental, 'Frozen Clouds' (3:33), continued the A-side's lyricism in a dream-like Johnson keyboard solo. On his website, Johnson revealed that the A-side title reflected his personal habits, visiting Bunhill Fields cemetery:

> I have often drunk my coffee by the grave of William Blake. On and off over the last 40 years, I have lived close by and have always found it an inspiring place to sit and meditate upon life. Nostalgia is part of the human condition, and change is inevitable in our lives and in the world around us. Large capital cities such as London often amplify the sense of change, although one thing that never seems to change is the cynicism of those in power.

Despite the heartfelt meanings in the lyrics, it's a very laid-back tune, with a rousing chorus: 'The sun hangs low, the church bells toll/The clouds unfold with burning gold/When truth breaks through these city walls/Perfidious

Albion must fall'. Backing vocals from Gillian Glover prove an apt counterpoint to Johnson's lead vocals against the background of soulful urban blues. The vivid imagery Johnson's velvet voice conjures plays well against the mesmerising instrumentation, including Sonya Cullingford's judiciously applied strings. A video of the band performing in a laid-back circle was shot by the stalwart Tim Pope.

'Zen & The Art Of Dating' 4:30
Proving Johnson had not lost his sense of humour following the overly serious opening tracks, 'Zen & The Art Of Dating' is a return to the pitfalls of modern romance. Like a fusion of 'Shrunken Man' and 'The Whisperers' from *Naked Self*, Johnson engages with internet app-driven dating with a wry line or two and a cutting comment focused on each of the sexes that are seeking real connection through a digital world of fleeting, superficial encounters. Here, Johnson revives his cod-MC character from *Dusk*'s 'True Happiness This Way Lies' as the omnipotent narrator of a story of the hunt for love in the digital age. There's a whimsical twist to both the tune and the lyrics, as the narrator swaps the female point of view for the male, each as forlorn as the other (accompanied by a burst of 'wah wah' guitar). There's something of a more tempered 'Dogs Of Lust' in lines like 'Breasts are yearning – loins are burning/Flirting with the point of no returning' and 'The fluid starts to rise/ That familiar throb deep inside'. The repeating chorus hook of 'Swipe to the left/Swipe to the right' is a witty take on internet dating, along with the threat of 'Endless lies, loveless coupling/The dance of strangers who'll never meet'. Johnson comes to an uplifting conclusion: 'Though it's a cliché, maybe it's true?/That only when you stop searching for love/Will love come searching for you'. A final 'Oh yeah' sends those in search of love off into the dark.

'Kissing The Ring Of POTUS' (Johnson, D. C. Collard) 3:33
Both dark and funny, 'Kissing The Ring Of POTUS' – a co-write between Johnson and keyboard king Collard – was an ideal song to present in the run-up to the contentious 2024 US general election in which Donald Trump secured a second term as President. Chronicling the downfall of 'the empire of lies' (that's the US, as if there's any doubt – 'a psychopathic superpower'), Johnson laments the rule of the neoliberal technocrats and career criminals (politicians, namely Trump) behind the 'coup that nobody noticed'. This harks back to *Mind Bomb*'s opening trio – 'Good Morning Beautiful', 'Armageddon Days (Are Here Again)' and 'The Violence Of Truth' – in focusing on American military and cultural domination. The lyrics are contained within a loose, bluesy tune that belies the subject matter. Not only were 'the criminals anointed', but 'By now so conceited and proud/They brag of their crimes out loud/"We cheated, we stole, we lied!"'. This may lack the punch of the bombastic 1980s production of *Mind Bomb*, being a more resigned laidback take on current affairs, but the lyrical conviction is just as strong. Johnson

continues to write as an outsider who loves much of America, while despising its rulers: 'So, is this how the Empire dies?/Its constitution withered on the vine/Propped up by the dollar and the drone/Slumped upon a degenerating throne'. His thematic concerns remain central, from the 1980s to the 2020s.

'Kissing the Ring of POTUS' was released as a digital single on 9 August 2025.

'Life After Life' 3:12

The first of a couple of tracks dealing with death and life after (see also 'Where Do We Go When We Die?'), 'Life After Life' engages with the idea of reincarnation, not new to Johnson's lyrics. *Mind Bomb*'s 'Gravitate To Me' climaxed with the lines: 'I know you/From a previous incarnation'. Having lost two brothers and both his parents, and now in his 60s, Johnson faces up to his own mortality. He conjures up another of The The's catchy, yet deep and meaningful couplets in the lines 'All the things you should have said but didn't say/All the things you could have done but didn't do', recalling those songs about ambition and failure like 'I've Been Waiting For Tomorrow (All Of My Life)' ('Another year over/And what have I done?') and 'The Sinking Feeling'. A second chance at life through reincarnation is suggested by the lines 'Remembering/Where you were, before you were you' and 'Those sirens on that distant shore/Tempting you back for more', suggesting that human souls are called back from the beyond (the album title *Ensoulment* refers to the moment when a being gains a soul). Johnson questions the forces that control life – 'But what really brought you to Earth?/But what really guided you from birth?' – before concluding with a twist: 'But the biggest clue with what is true?/Your thoughts are thinking – you!' Inspired by death and grief, 'Life After Life' (the title chanted by Glover) suggests there is life not only after but also before death, a consolation for those who have lost loved ones without invoking organised religion, which Johnson has railed against. Musically, 'Life After Life' is one of the best tracks here, feeling like an escapee from *Dusk*, and showing that Johnson has not lost his touch for meaningful lyrics.

Like much of *Ensoulment*, there's a blues-influenced yet relaxed approach, with Johnson himself providing electric and acoustic guitar, backed by Eller's bass. Terry Edward's horns add some uplifting high notes, while Earl Harvin's drums and Danny Cumming's percussion provide a solid backbeat. It's one of the band's best tracks, coming from a more mature group of musicians.

'I Want To Wake Up With You' 4:00

Closing what would have been side one, Johnson returns to his own young adulthood with 'I Want To Wake Up With You', a song about the desires of youth ('Though not a boy/Barely a man') and the closest this album comes to a love song (previous albums usually boasted two or three). A series of songs on *Ensoulment* deal with memory and the act of remembrance, from the changing London of 'William Blake' to the childhood lament of 'Down By The

Frozen River' that opens side two. 'Risin' Above The Need' recalls Johnson's own addictions of the 1990s, while 'I Hope You Remember (The Things I Can't Forget)' tackles the outsourcing of memory to social media. It was a topic Johnson tackled with *Flood* magazine: 'That song isn't about one particular relationship; it's a composite of different situations. It's really about that moment where two people are falling in love, that moment just before, when it's a recognition on both sides of this attraction, and the walls dissolving between them. I think it's a feeling that people spend their lives trying to experience.' Nostalgia is a frequent topic in The The songs (for example, 'Weather Belle' on *Naked Self*: 'Nostalgia strikes hard at the heart/That cannot escape its past'), but here it's seen as a negative: 'Nostalgia's got this habit of blowing back'. It's a song on a knife edge between positivity ('Bodies bared, confidences shared/ You held my eyes, we longingly stared') and the negative ('falling out of love/ With its soul-searching cleanse/I got what I wanted, but I lost what I had'). There's also a play with the idea of the world as a hallucination, as the title is abbreviated to a closing lament of 'I want to wake up'.

Dominated by Collard's floating keyboards and Harvin's slow-going drums, it's a contemplative track, downplaying Barrie Cadogan's electric guitar and James Eller's acoustic bass in favour of Johnson's storytelling vocals. Things take a woozy turn towards the end, however, as the guitars are distorted, suggesting a nightmare rather than a dream, with a buried in the mix laugh wrapping things up.

'Down By The Frozen River' (Johnson, Collard) 3:33

More a poem narrated against Collard's piano, 'Down By The Frozen River' is mostly a recalling of a 1960s British childhood, complete with truanting, gang fights and drinking illicit alcohol in the woods – a standard experience that persisted well into the 1980s. It's an odd track, unless it is looked at in conjunction with *The Inertia Variations* narration that Johnson produced as part of the *Radio Cineola Trilogy*. Johnson has a great voice for narration, one that would not be out of place on Radio 4 nor on an audiobook narration. While sections of previous songs had sometimes given way to narrations ('True Happiness Lies This Way' kicks off *Dusk* with one), it's not the norm for The The. That makes 'Down By The Frozen River' stand out, and come across as more of an indulgence, a personal expression resulting from misplaced nostalgia, rather than an engagement with what's happening now. It is only at the end that Johnson ties in the politics of the rest of the album. He can't help himself, expressing his own lack of formal education and autodidactism as preferable to being 'programmed' by the state: 'But, over-educated to the point of stupidity/Many lost their spirit as well as their liberty' and 'Faced with a future, to which my kind is consigned/I escaped with an empty head, but an open mind'. This is accompanied by a blues-style piano riff from Collard and horns from Terry Edwards (who also featured on 'Kissing The Ring of POTUS').

'Risin' Above The Need' 3:46

Johnson deals with addiction in a hopeful way on 'Risin' Above The Need' (released as a double A-side single with 'Where Do We Go When We Die?'), a song that sees a mature artist look back upon his past behaviour, feeling relief that he's changed: 'Stripped of my addictions and deceit/I'm feeling somewhat … incomplete/Y'see, too much was never enough for me'. Bluesy guitar underpins this, giving the whole thing an oddly 1970s vibe. It's one of the most catchy cuts on *Ensoulment*, and one of the more accessible. It's a track that comes across as a refugee from *Dusk*. There are perennial The The concerns here, such as 'That thin line between satisfaction and greed/When what we want ain't really what we need' and 'But all good things will come through the door/To those who do not want them … anymore'. It's a beautiful track, creating uplifting music from a period when Johnson recognised he'd gone too far, as he told *The Guardian*: '[Fame] left a trail of destruction in my personal life because, for a while, it went to my head … Drugs. Alcohol. Being disrespectful. My partner walked out on me, and I worked very hard to get her back, and it was a hard lesson. Fame is like inhaling a toxic substance.' All those 'toxic substances' lie behind 'Risin' Above The Need', putting a positive spin on a negative inspiration. The track was released as a double A-sided single (with 'Where Do We Go When We Die?') in December 2024.

'Linoleum Smooth To The Stockinged Foot' 3:53 (3:38, single edit)

Is 'Linoleum Smooth...' a COVID conspiracy song or simply a diary account of a strange event in Johnson's life? Inspired by his hallucinogenic hospital stay when being treated for his voice-threatening pharyngeal abscess, the song was perhaps not the wisest choice for a single. It opens in a psychedelic, dissonant manner, the kind of noises not heard since *Burning Blue Soul*. Johnson's lyrics suggest that 'the truth' can be glimpsed in 'altered states', while 'High priests in white lab coats/Evangelise the disease as the antidote'. Edwards' horns and Cullingford's strings add to the nightmarish dissonance of an eerie horror movie soundtrack, as it builds its political points: 'Driven idiotic with fear/Dissenters are herded, then smeared'.

Like the points Johnson thinks he's making, the track descends into a cacophony of noise, a slather of nonsense that suggests those in power during the COVID-19 pandemic were somehow actually 'demonic'; this is too close to some right-wing talking points for comfort. In 2020, Johnson had appeared to back wild internet conspiracies about the pandemic: in a tweet since deleted, Johnson made reference to *The Corbett Report* podcast, which gave credence to the notion that Bill Gates was involved with the genesis of COVID. While the theory of a lab origin for the virus is perfectly valid, the notion of an international conspiracy to subjugate populations through fear seems rather farfetched – after all, it didn't work and things returned to what passes for normality rather more quickly than most anticipated. It was a successful single, though, reaching a peak of number five on the UK Vinyl

Singles Chart. The B-side, titled 'Mycelium Muse' (4:08), is another atmospheric, film soundtrack-like instrumental, continuing the dissonant sounds of the A-side and featuring subtle fiddle work from Sonja Cullingford and ambient horns by Terry Edwards.

'Linoleum Smooth...' captures a moment in time, when Johnson was out of his head on drugs and open to influence. As he told *The Guardian*: 'Because I'd been given morphine, I was thinking that maybe I'd actually died and this was a halfway house. My instinct was to get myself moving. So, I'd be pacing the wards in surgical stockings with a drip, thinking: 'I've got to get a song out of this."

'Where Do We Go When We Die?' 4:02
Another reincarnation song, 'Where Do We Go When We Die?' is more solemn than the almost upbeat 'Life After Life' and was written in response to the death of Johnson's publican father, Eddie. Everything comes together – Johnson's lyrics and voice, Cadogan and Eller's guitars, Harvin's drums, Cullingford's strings and Danny Cummings' percussion – to produce a hugely emotional track in a distinctive musical style that only The The can manage. Again, the question of life after death is raised, but there are few answers. As Johnson's lyrics maintain: 'But what's the point of life/If we can never die?' It is perhaps Johnson's most mature song, dealing with mortality, with those who've gone and those left behind. Johnson doesn't have any answers, but he is a seeker, always looking for hope, 'seeking proof/searching for signs'. Johnson movingly concludes: 'And as the river flows back into the sea/Then so shall we...' perhaps to be reborn one day...

'I Hope You Remember (The Things I Can't Forget)' (Johnson, Cadogan) 3:38
Adopting the style of a troubadour or musical vaudeville, Johnson and Co. adopt the guise of a working-class balladeer raging against the domination of the machines, as they slowly replace our memories. Accompanied by clapping and stomping, the song explores 'the experiences that money cannot buy', the kind of personal reminiscences that the machines cannot conjure. Chronicling the machines moving in 'to correct our faults/assist our living/think our thoughts', Johnson laments the passing of the sense memories of his youth: perfume, tobacco smoke, 'penny chews' and 'coal tar soap'. Before the end, 'I Hope You Remember...' turns into another meditation on life after death and the possibility of reincarnation: 'More than just the molecules that animate our flesh/We are eternal beings, sempiternally blessed/Free as the day we die, pure as we are born/Our souls remain deathless, no need to mourn'. Johnson envisages the human spirit or soul as being eternal ('sempiternally blessed'), perhaps changing form but forever lasting. It's a hopeful, uplifting message, and either this or 'Where Do We Go When We Die?' could have provided a fitting last track for *Ensoulment*, but Johnson had one more surprise up his sleeve...

'A Rainy Day In May' 3:59

A call-back to *Dusk*'s 'Weather Belle', 'A Rainy Day In May' is a relationship song that doesn't even get as far as a one-night stand. Spinning the scene setting of 'Weather Belle' into a whole song, Johnson considers the meeting of souls across a train carriage as a couple lock eyes, don't even meet or speak, but part, wondering what might have happened if things had been different. It's the most lyrically simple track on *Ensoulment*, recalling some of Johnson's past greats. The humming harmony between verses gives it ethereal life, a wondering tone: 'You caught my gaze/I swooned/Your eyes touched every part of my wound/The other half of my soul/Welcoming me home'. It's a melancholy end, a song of unrequited feelings, of unformed longings, of lost opportunities. Sonya Cullingford's emotional fiddle work is the subtle cherry on top, bringing *Ensoulment* to a satisfying conclusion, with an extended instrumental finish that too few of the earlier tracks on *Ensoulment* exhibit. Johnson's higher register 'woo hoo'-ing gives way to the kind of abstract drone that introduced 'Cognitive Dissident', bringing things full circle.

Related Tracks
'We Can't Stop What's Coming' 4:03

A product of the recording in May 2016 of other artists covering The The songs, 'We Can't Stop What's Coming' had been written in response to the loss of Johnson's brother, Andrew. Both James Eller and Johanna St Michaels (recording the event as part of *The Inertia Variations* film) suggested Johnson perform the new song. Johnson hadn't performed in public for 14 years, since the Meltdown event at the Royal Festival Hall in 2002, and there was some doubt throughout the day whether he would actually do so. The band and others involved didn't know whether he would perform as Johnson wasn't sure himself until the last minute. Talking to *The Guardian*, Johnson confessed: 'So many people have asked me: 'What were you thinking about?' I was thinking: 'Please let me remember the first line.'' Those watching the internet broadcast live were rewarded when Johnson summoned up his courage and stepped to the microphone to sing.

The track saw a wider release for Record Store Day in 2017 as a single-sided 7" single in a limited run of just 2000 copies, the first new The The single in 15 years. Further copies – without the Andrew Johnson image etched on the B-side – were released in June to meet demand, with 50% of the profits going to the St Nicholas Hospice, where Andrew spent his final days.

Although the song was specifically about the loss of Andrew, the lyrics gave it far wider relevance. Playing on the single were Johnny Marr, James Eller, Chris Whitten on drums, and Iain Berryman on keyboards, with backing vocals from Meja Kullerstein. Even shorn of its context, it is a moving piece, with the video made up from family home movies featuring Matt and Andrew and clips from past The The videos. Perhaps Johnson was thinking of it as his own swan song at the time, with lyrics like 'Silence from your songs/Reminds us, when you are gone' being equally applicable to his own long absence. The passage of time – so often a The The obsession – features here: 'We can't hate the river for flowing/Can't blame the wild wind blowin'/Can't slow the time from running' while Johnson personified Andrew's cancer with the words: 'Inside a shadow that grows/A darkness in the darkness/A stranger on the shore'.

If Johnson felt 'We Can't Stop...' was to be his final word, his fans had a different idea. The overwhelming response, proving that he still had a dedicated audience waiting for new music, set Johnson on the road to the 2018 *Comeback Special* tour and, ultimately, to the 2024 album *Ensoulment*. It is a pivotal The The track.

'I Want 2 B U' 3:20
This song emerged from the soundtrack Johnson had written for his brother Gerard's 2019 film *Muscle*. As with 'We Can't Stop What's Coming', it was issued as a Record Store Day single for August 2020, backed with 'Velvet Muscle Scream' (3:45, a crunchy cut underpinned by machine-like percussion, driven by synth drones). Opening the soundtrack album, 'I Want 2 B U' is an instantly catchy tune, utilising his trademark Omnichord for the first time since 1983's 'This Is The Day'. Heavily relying on the 'la-la-la-la' vocals, Johnson included a few spicy bon mots, including the ominous 'Truth is nothing but a point of view' that would inform much of *Ensoulment*, and the reflection on his past life with 'Always searching for another high/Tryna catch up with lost time', and there are unmistakable echoes of past The The classics in the line 'The love of fear/the fear of love'. It's not as poignant as 'We Can't Stop...', but 'I Want 2 B U' was a palate cleanser, allowing Johnson to continue to move forward with his re-engagement with songwriting after so long away. The track was disassembled and stitched back together as 'Want U 2 B I' on the *Muscle* soundtrack.

'$1 One Vote!' 3:57
The third new The The single in six years, '$1 One Vote' emerged from an earlier version under the more confrontational title 'Justice 4 Jesus'. As Johnson confirmed: 'It is a song that has been percolating for a number of years. I was always having trouble finding the right words to finish it off, but the nascent dystopia of the last couple of years has certainly opened eyes, sharpened minds and clarified thoughts.'

Featuring art from the late Andy 'Dog' Johnson of a malevolent teeth-baring Mickey Mouse, the February 2023 release engaged with the culture of identity politics. There were COVID-related lines such as 'While all the diseases/Are too lucrative to cure/Too much to endure' and much concern with questions of truth: 'Even truth in an age of deceit/Is impossible to believe' and 'What was said is unsaid/What's implied is denied/Fact becomes opinion/Opinion becomes crime' – a take that was followed up in 'Cognitive Dissident'. Another target for Johnson was the 'be kind' community that nonetheless attacks those who disagree with them, highlighted by the powerful lines: 'Those who profess love the loudest/Practice hate the proudest'.

Driven by an insistent guitar line (recurring on the chorus), the track has an aggressive opening, switching to a slower, more tuneful approach. It has an unusual structure to go along with the unusual lyrics: 'There ain't no cure for this virus of the mind'. Some worried that Johnson had succumbed to internet-driven conspiracy theories (and some of the tracks on *Ensoulment* would reinforce those views), but Johnson has always been a contrarian, a dissident who went his own way – similar sentiments can be found in songs on *Soul Mining*, *Infected*, *Mind Bomb* and *Dusk*. As he concluded (echoing a then-ongoing political campaign): 'Time to take back what we own!' The B-side offered a physical release for 'Mrs Mac' (2:32). With '$1 One Vote!', The The were truly back.

Bibliography

Books
Doyle, Wesley, *Conform To Deform: The Weird And Wonderful World of Some Bizzare* (Jawbone Press, 2023).
Fraser, Neil, *Long Shadows, High Hopes* (Omnibus Press, 2018, 2022).
Somers, Thierry (Editor), *The 2018 Comeback Special Official Tour Book* (Lazarus/Cineloa, 2018).

Websites
thethe.com [Matt Johnson], *keithsneuroblog.blogspot.com* [Keith Laws], *wewantthetheback.fandom.com*, *the-the-co.fandom.com*, *djfood.org*, *wesleydoylewrites.substack.com*, *peoplelikeus.org*, *colinlloydtucker.com*, *forums.stevehoffman.tv*, *tapeop.com*, *the guardian.com*, *thequietus.com*, *floodmagazine.com*, *theartsdesk.com*, *thevinylfactory.com*, *uncut.co.uk*, *discogs.com*, *themouthmagazine.com*, *pastemagazine.com*, *nme.com*, *pitchfork.com*, *electronicsound.co.uk*, *trouserpress.com*, *postpunk.com*, *telegraph.co.uk*, *americansongwriter.com*, *postpunkmonk.com*, *rollingstone.com*, *chaoscontrol.com*, *200-percent.com*, *lloydcole.com*, *scotsman.com*, *clashmusic.com*, *martinbelam.com*, *theransomnote.com*, *dazeddigital.com*, *withguitars.com*, *slicingupeyeballs.com*, *obladada.com*, *magnetmagazine.com*, *albumoftheyear.org*, *thatericalper.com*, *rave-and-roll.com*, *avforums.com*, *randophonic.com*, *goldenplec.com*, *popsike.com*, *whatsmyscene.com*, *nostalgiacentral.com*, *antiestablishment.bandcamp.com*, *songsmiths.wordpress.com*, *irishtimes.com*, *independent.co.uk*, *faroutmagazine.co.uk*, *spillmagazine.com*, *mojo4music.com*, *glidemagazine.com*, *recordcollectormag.com*, *twostorymelody.com*, *popmatters.com*, *softoctopus.co.uk*, *morrissey-solo.com*, *arcticreviews.co.uk*, *forum.popjustice.com*, *dangerousminds.net*, *bigtakeover.com*, *sun-13.com*, *wakemag.org*, *latimes.com*, *besteveralbums.com*, *thatrecordgotmehigh.com*, *outsideleft.com*, *classicalbumsundays.com*, *rockandrollclobe.com*, *Wikipedia*, *imdb.com*, *officialcharts.com*, *medium.com*, *reddit.com*, *bbc.co.uk* [BBC Sounds], *youtube.com*